Louisiana

Louisiana

Martin Hintz

Children's Press®
A Division of Grolier Publishing
New York London Hong Kong Sydney
Danbury, Connecticut

Frontispiece: A slow-moving Louisiana bayou
Front cover: The French Quarter, New Orleans
Back cover: Passenger steamer at sunset
on the Mississippi River

Consultant: Judy Smith, Louisiana State Library

Please note: All statistics are as up-to-date as possible at the time of publication.

Visit Children's Press on the Internet at http://publishing.grolier.com

Book production by Editorial Directions, Inc.

Library of Congress Cataloging-in-Publication Data

Hintz, Martin.
    Louisiana / by Martin Hintz.
      p. cm. — (America the beautiful. Second series)
    Includes bibliographical references (p.) and index.
    Summary : Describes the history, geography, ecology, people, economy, cities,
and sights of the Pelican State of Louisiana.
    ISBN 0-516-20634-6
    Louisiana—Juvenile literature. [1. Louisiana.] I. Title. II. Series.
F369.3.H56 1998
976.3—dc21
                                                      98-11032
                                                      CIP
                                                       AC

Acknowledgments

For their advice, assistance, and good cheer, the author wishes to thank Bruce Morgan, director of communications for the Office of Tourism, Louisiana Department of Culture, Recreation and Tourism; historian Bennett H. Wall; Beverly Gianna and her staff at the New Orleans Metropolitan Visitor and Convention Center; Gerard Breaux and his staff at the Lafayette Convention and Visitors Bureau; and all the other Louisianians who shared their life stories and their community histories. They included waitresses, police dispatchers, fishers, boat operators, corporate executives, tourism officials, musicians, politicians, actors, shopkeepers, cab drivers, grounds attendants, museum curators, artists, and even a juggler, mime, and steamboat pilot or two.

Mardi Gras

Mississippi riverboat

Cajun musician

Street musician
in New Orleans

Contents

Offshore oil platform

Kisatachie National Forest

Strawberries

Statue of Evangeline in St. Martinville

CHAPTER ONE

Hello to Louisiana

The French Quarter
of New Orleans

The airboat skips across the bayou. Towering cypress trees, their branches draped with Spanish moss, rear up from the water. Muskrat homes dot the backwater where an egret rises gracefully. Near the bank, an alligator watches from the swamp grass.

A torrent of drumming comes from the open door of a night-club, while a dance club in New Orleans's French Quarter gives just a hint of the boom-boom action going on inside. Nearby, five boys tap-dance on the sidewalk.

A towboat makes its way down the muddy Mississippi River past barges filled with corn.

Along the New Orleans waterfront, the river traffic chugs past the city. In the World Trade Center, a company vice president

Opposite: Moss-draped cypress trees line the bank of Lacassine Bayou near Hayes, Louisiana.

**Geopolitical map of
Louisiana**

swivels around in her office chair. During the 1850s, her ancestors were slaves. Her great-grandmother could not read or write. Her grandmother was the first in her family to graduate from high school. Today, this woman directs operations for a multinational corporation.

A souvenir shop has a colorful display of Mardi Gras masks, stuffed alligators, and posters. The owner came to Louisiana from Vietnam in the 1980s. This is his third family-run store.

A young boy and his father have come to the Mansfield State Commemorative Area to see a battlefield reenactment. Already the troops are marching out to their lines. Afterward, the boy and his father will talk about the 1864 battle in which 26,000 Union troops were turned back by a Confederate army of 8,000 men.

This is Louisiana—old and new, raucous and reflective, a wonderful state. From its ancient history to its modern bustle, Louisiana has plenty of everything.

During the festival of Mardi Gras, people in masks and costumes parade through the streets.

CHAPTER TWO

Louisiana Is Born

eople have lived in Louisiana for thousands of years. Artifacts found on Avery Island date back to at least 700 B.C., and there is evidence that the early Louisiana culture predated the Maya and Inca of South America.

The remains of ancient villages are found throughout the state. The soil—perfect for crops—and the abundance of wildlife and waterways attracted early residents.

These clay artifacts found at the Poverty Point mound were probably used to heat water.

The Mound Builders

Numerous mounds built by the early people dot Louisiana. Many mounds have been looted during the past century, but others are now protected by the state. They yield everything from pottery to fishhooks. The mounds are 50 to more than 200 feet (15 to 61 m) in length and width and range from 5 to more than 50 feet (2 to 15 m) high.

The lowest mounds were used for burials and located near the villages. Middens were simply garbage dumps where the people piled up their trash. Temple mounds—the highest—were used in ancient rituals.

Opposite: Arrow points made by Louisiana's early people

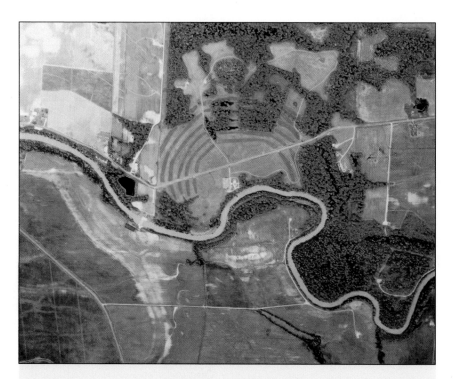

A Temple Mound

The bird-shaped mound at Poverty Point is the second-largest Native American mound in the United States. It stands more than 70 feet (21 m) high. (An aerial view is shown above.) Numerous effigies of birds found in the mound suggest that the mound builders may have worshiped these small bird statues. The Poverty Point mound was built at least 3,000 years ago, with the highest point of the earthen structure representing the "head" of the bird.

Inhabitants of the region were skilled craftspeople who made pottery and other artifacts years before their neighbors. Studies of these early people at Poverty Point began in 1913. ■

The Chitimacha

The 280-acre (113-ha) Chitimacha Indian Reservation in Charenton near Baldwin is now part of Jean Lafitte National Historical

Park and Preserve. The word *chitimacha* means "men altogether red." The tribe has lived in the area for centuries, and when the Acadians, French-speaking refugees from Canada, arrived in the 1700s, the cultures merged through intermarriage. The reservation, however, is still home to 190 of the Chitimacha tribe's 500-plus registered members. Anyone who can prove one-sixteenth Chitimacha blood can become a registered tribal member.

The reservation has a museum, park, trading post, school, and other community buildings, including a bingo hall that is run by a British company. Each year, around the Fourth of July, the tribe hosts a Green Corn Festival.

The Atakapa

Among the Native American people who once called Louisiana their home were the Atakapa. They were hunters and gatherers who used their environment with respect. Through the centuries, they traded with other tribes hundreds of miles away. Shells, dried fish, skins, copper, pearls, pottery, and baskets from Louisiana have been found throughout central North America.

The Wildlife

The fertile soil and abundance of wildlife in northern Louisiana supported large numbers of Native Americans and kept them close to home. In southern Louisiana, Indian families lived on hillocks of dry ground amid the swamps. Their open-sided huts, made of palmetto leaves and reeds, invited fresh breezes on hot, muggy nights. They slept in hammocks or on raised platforms to protect themselves from snakes and alligators.

Hernando de Soto

Hernando de Soto was born in Spain around 1500. He took part in the Spanish invasions of Panama and Nicaragua and helped Francisco Pizarro in his attack on the Aztec. De Soto became wealthy from the treasure he looted, but he wanted more. He wanted fame.

King Charles V of Spain named de Soto governor of Cuba in 1537. From there, he organized an expedition to Florida. Leading a force of 600 soldiers, he came to what is now the American coast and eventually made his way to the Mississippi River. He died of a fever on May 21, 1542. ■

De Soto Arrives

Spaniard Hernando de Soto was the first European to explore what is now Louisiana. In 1541 and 1542, he led soldiers, slaves, and missionaries through Arkansas and into northern Louisiana.

French Exploration

For almost 100 years, Louisiana was neglected by the European powers. In 1682, however, French explorer René-Robert Cavelier, Sieur de la Salle, claimed the Mississippi Valley for France. La Salle called this region Louisiana in honor of Louis XIV, the king of France.

In 1699, another French explorer—Pierre Le Moyne, Sieur d'Iberville—founded the royal French colony of Louisiana.

D'Iberville traveled northward as far as present-day Baton Rouge, which he named after seeing a red stick that marked the territory of two Indian nations. (*Baton rouge* means "red stick" in French.) The French spent the next few years building forts along the Gulf Coast. In the meantime, King Louis XIV died, and his

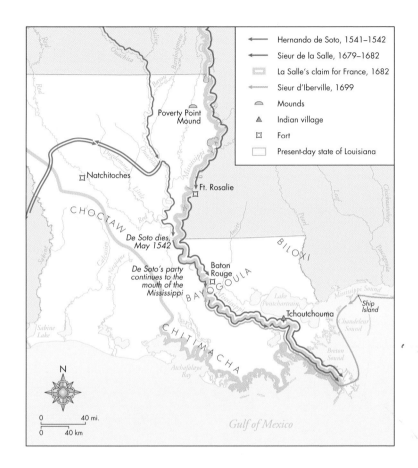

Map legend:
- ← Hernando de Soto, 1541–1542
- ← Sieur de la Salle, 1679–1682
- La Salle's claim for France, 1682
- ← Sieur d'Iberville, 1699
- ⌒ Mounds
- ▲ Indian village
- ⌂ Fort
- ☐ Present-day state of Louisiana

Poverty Point Mound

Natchitoches

Ft. Rosalie

CHOCTAW

De Soto dies, May 1542

De Soto's party continues to the mouth of the Mississippi

Baton Rouge

BILOXI

BAYOGOULA

Tchoutchouma

Ship Island

CHITIMACHA

Atchafalaya Bay

Sabine Lake

N

0   40 mi.
0   40 km

Gulf of Mexico

Scottish financier
John Law

five-year-old great-grandchild took the crown as Louis XV. Louis's uncle—Philippe II, Duc d'Orléans—was then named regent (ruler).

The Mississippi Bubble

A Scottish financier and speculator named John Law gained the confidence of Philippe II and got his permission to colonize Louisiana. In 1717, Law was given a twenty-five-year charter that allowed him to do almost anything, but he needed people in the colony so that he could start making money. His agents went all over Europe looking for anyone desperate enough to seek a new life overseas. Law fired the first Louisiana governor and installed Jean-Baptiste Le Moyne, Sieur de Bienville—younger brother of d'Iberville—as his puppet governor. Law sold worthless stock to wealthy Europeans to raise money for the colony in a venture that became known as the Mississippi Bubble.

New Orleans

Few people were eager to go to Louisiana, even with all Law's promises, so prisons were emptied, with judges sentencing "death or Louisiana." In 1718, Bienville came across the Indian village of Tchoutchouma, between Lake Pontchartrain and the Mississippi River. It looked like a good site for a town, so he built a stockade there and called it *Nouvelle Orléans* (New Orleans) after the Duc d'Orléans. That village became the capital of Louisiana in 1722.

An artist's rendering of the city of New Orleans as it looked in 1718

The Acadians

A flood of land-hungry settlers soon arrived from Germany, France, and other European countries. In 1764, 4,000 French settlers, known as Acadians, arrived after being expelled from their homes in Acadia, eastern Canada, by the British. Their descendants came to be known as Cajuns.

The French Need Money

The French needed more money than the early colony could provide. They turned Louisiana over to the Spanish in a secret 1762 treaty to prevent the colony from falling into British hands. To keep the peace, the local French in Louisiana, called Creoles, were not told of the takeover until 1764. When the Spanish arrived, however, the French rebelled. One Spanish governor, Alexander O'Reilly, was actually an Irish soldier of fortune. He was so ruthless in putting down the French revolt in 1769 that he was called "Bloody O'Reilly."

Don Bernardo de Galvez, governor of Louisiana during Spanish rule

During the American Revolution (1775–1783), the Spanish controlled Louisiana and Florida, effectively blocking the British from both areas. After the war, the Spanish and the victorious Americans signed the Treaty of San Lorenzo, which guaranteed various trade allowances and opened the port of New Orleans and the lower Mississippi River to even more trade.

When Napoléon Bonaparte came to power in France, he convinced his weaker Spanish neighbors to return Louisiana to France. This was done under the Treaty of San Ildefonso in 1800. All this geographical maneuvering among European powers made U.S. President Thomas Jefferson extremely nervous. Jefferson sent

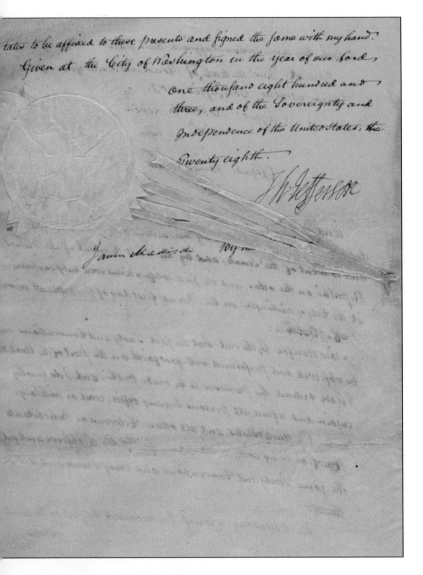

envoys to France to arrange a land deal, hoping to buy the west Florida area and the land around New Orleans.

Napoléon Sells Louisiana

When it came to money, Napoléon was willing to listen. He had overextended his armies in Europe and needed cash to continue fighting. Napoléon sold all of Louisiana for only $15 million in 1803. The territory consisted of most of western North America, from Canada to the Gulf of Mexico. Considered one of the best land deals in history, the Louisiana Purchase doubled the size of the United States and set the country on its way to becoming a powerful nation.

The document authorizing the Louisiana Purchase, signed by Thomas Jefferson and James Madison

The Florida Parishes

While these negotiations were going on, Spain still claimed the "Florida Parishes," the land east of the Mississippi River and north of Lakes Maurepas and Pontchartrain. Several treaties were needed later to confirm the territorial boundaries of Louisiana. In 1804, Congress divided the huge territory to make it easier to govern. One part was called the Louisiana Territory and was later termed the Missouri Territory. The other part was named the Territory of Orleans and later became the state of Louisiana.

The Creoles Object

The transfer of Louisiana to the United States after the Louisiana Purchase of 1803 was not good news for the French-speaking Creoles, especially in New Orleans. The American newcomers were a wild bunch who got into many duels with the well-established French residents, but each nationality needed the other for business reasons. As a result, wide tracts of land in New Orleans were declared "neutral grounds," where fighting was forbidden. The median strips that separate busy traffic lanes in New Orleans today are still called "neutral grounds."

Historical map of Louisiana

A Creole Wedding

Many Louisiana Creoles were wealthy. They controlled the plantations, the river traffic, and the urban business life. One Creole especially noted for his rich lifestyle was Charles Durand. Durand built Pine Alley plantation, one of the most beautiful properties in the South, near the calm waters of Bayou Teche.

When two of his daughters were married on the same day, Durand imported spiders from China to spin webs on 3 miles (5 km) of trees leading to his house. His slaves sprinkled gold and silver dust on the dew-speckled webs early that morning, creating a fairyland effect for the wedding guests. ■

West Florida

Danger of another war loomed in 1810 when American settlers in the Florida Parishes rebelled against Spain. West Florida declared itself independent on September 26, and Baton Rouge, the seat of the Spanish government, was captured by the revolutionaries. When West Florida proclaimed itself a republic, the Spanish quickly retreated to Pensacola, Florida. President James Madison undercut this move toward independence by declaring West Florida part of the United States and sending his own administrators to govern the region.

From Territory to State

The census of 1810 showed that the territory was now eligible for admission to the Union as a state. At the time, 76,556 people lived in the area. But the Yankees of the northern states, called Federalists, were suspicious of the French population of Louisiana. After all, they reasoned, these "foreigners" had different customs and

The Creoles and the Americans

After the Louisiana Purchase, the differences between the two national personalities in the Territory of Orleans were especially noticeable in New Orleans. The Americans lived near the modern Lafayette Square, while the French-speaking Creoles resided around the historical Place d'Armes (now known as Jackson Square).

The Creole social and business life swirled around the St. Louis Hotel, while the Americans gathered at the Hotel St. Charles. Creole mansions stood along the Esplanade, while the Americans built their palatial houses on St. Charles Street. The Americans worshiped in St. Patrick's Church, while the Creoles went to St. Louis Cathedral. These architecturally rich neighborhoods and imposing landmarks can still be seen. ◾

spoke a different language. But wiser heads in Congress authorized a territorial assembly, which was like a legislature. The assembly was to prepare for a special election to name a state constitutional convention. Eventually, forty-five delegates representing nineteen counties met in New Orleans in 1811 and drew up a constitution. On April 30, 1812, Louisiana became the eighteenth state.

CHAPTER THREE

Louisiana Faces Challenges

t the time Louisiana became part of the Union, the United States faced many challenges. Almost immediately, the new state was swept up in the War of 1812 (1812–1815), which raged between the United States and Britain. The war broke out when the United States objected to Britain seizing its ships on the high seas and conscripting its sailors into the Royal Navy. In addition, people in the northwestern United States were meeting armed resistance when they tried to take more land from the Indians there. They believed the Indians were getting British support.

The Army Invades

The war's fury spread over the country. In the north, when American troops invaded Canada and burned its capital city of York, the British retaliated by burning Washington, D.C. In the deep South, the Creek Indian nation was engaged in a life-and-death struggle with American soldiers led by General Andrew Jackson. Jackson, however, eventually defeated the Creek in 1814. Jackson then moved down to New Orleans, where an army of British veterans was about to storm ashore and take the city.

As it happened, the war was already over when this tragic situation unfolded. Sailing ships were speeding across the Atlantic with welcome news that a peace treaty had been signed in Ghent,

Pirate Jean Lafitte joined American troops, Choctaw Indians, free blacks, and slaves in the fight against the British.

Opposite: General Andrew Jackson led troops to victory in Louisiana during the War of 1812.

Belgium. But the news was late in reaching far-off Louisiana, and neither side knew the war was over. So, in December 1814, General Jackson arrived in New Orleans with his ragtag army of sharpshooters. They joined white Louisiana militia, free blacks and slaves, Choctaw Indians, and local civilians of all ages who picked up muskets and swords to defend their homes. A band of pirates even offered to fight alongside the Americans in exchange for a pardon. The pirates had been preying on ships in the Gulf of Mexico. Jackson gladly accepted the services of these pirates, led by Jean Lafitte, a former New Orleans blacksmith.

The Army Comes Ashore

After defeating five American gunboats, the British fleet sailed to within 7 miles (11 km) of New Orleans and put its army ashore.

The Battle of New Orleans

General Edward Pakenham, an Irishman fighting for the British, expected an easy victory on January 8, 1815. Instead, dozens of exhausted, wet, and muddy soldiers were killed as they marched through the cypress swamps. Later, in the New Orleans suburb of Chalmette, steely-eyed marksmen hid behind cotton bales and overturned wagons, where they had no trouble picking off the closely packed ranks of British soldiers. One of Lafitte's gunners, Dominique You, directed the American artillery with devastating effect. Within a few minutes, General Pakenham was killed, along with 300 to 400 of his men. An additional 1,700 men were wounded and 500 reported missing. Most of those missing soldiers probably sank beneath the surface of the foul-smelling swamp waters. The Americans suffered only 71 casualties.

Business Booms

After the war, business boomed in Louisiana. Traders took advantage of the newest form of transportation—the steamboat. Previously, keelboats loaded with cargo were floated downstream to New Orleans and then dismantled for their wood. Sailboats had a hard time going back upstream, and trips took three to four months. A steamboat could carry large amounts of goods up and down the mighty Mississippi River in five or six days.

A steamboat traveling the Mississippi River into the port of New Orleans, 1880

Mississippi Steamboats

Mississippi River steamboats were as luxurious as ocean liners. They had three decks mounted above a flat-bottomed hull that allowed them to dock almost anywhere and a long plank that swung out from the deck to let passengers board.

The main deck was used for machinery, cargo, and passengers. The middle deck was reserved for higher-paying passengers and officers. The "texas" deck was the highest; it was the vantage point from which the pilot steered the vessel.

Some steamboats had stern paddle wheels to propel the boat through the water, and others had wheels mounted on the sides.

Although these boats were rugged, the trips were often dangerous. Sometimes boilers exploded as captains raced each other to the next port. Shifting sandbars and hidden rocks could rip out the bottom of a boat in a minute. Only a few passenger-carrying steamboats still travel along the Mississippi today. ■

The *New Orleans,* the first steamboat to dock in New Orleans, arrived in 1812 from Pittsburgh via the Ohio and Mississippi Rivers. In 1814, 21 vessels arrived, and by 1840, there were 400. Cargo tonnage also made a huge leap during that time—increasing from 67,560 to 537,000 tons. New Orleans became the fourth-largest city in the United States and the second-largest port, after New York.

State Benefits

The entire state benefited from this commercial spurt. More land was opened for settlement when the Caddo Indians sold their Louisiana land. Planters from the poorer southern states flocked to the region, drawn by the rich soil that was great for growing cotton. They also wanted access to the rivers for timely delivery of their cargoes. The towns of Shreveport and Alexandria quickly became commercial powerhouses.

Overland trade routes to the southwest were as important as the rivers. People there also needed goods provided by the United States. Many Louisianians moved to the Mexican territories of Texas, New Mexico, and Arizona in the 1830s and 1840s in another great Western migration.

Trouble in Texas

Texas wanted to break away from Mexican control, however, and on March 2, 1836, adopted a declaration of independence. American business and political leaders also wanted this vast territory, so they flocked to Texas to join the fray. Texas general Sam Houston eventually defeated Mexican general Santa Anna at San Jacinto on April 21, 1836, and independence was won. The Republic of Texas lasted from 1836 until December 29, 1845, when Texas was admitted to the Union. Mexico threatened to go to war over the annexation of Texas, so General Zachary Taylor was ordered to the Rio Grande with 4,000 troops.

The Mexicans refused to meet with American diplomats, saying the presence of American troops aggravated the situation. Fighting broke out, and the U.S. forces invaded—and eventually defeated—Mexico.

The Filibusters

After the Mexican War (1846–1848), New Orleans was considered a perfect base for launching attacks on Cuba and other countries by adventure-seeking Americans who wanted to invade these regions. Such people were called "filibusters." Narcisco Lopez organized two expeditions from New Orleans in a failed

Yellow Fever

The dreaded disease known as yellow fever, or "yellow jack," killed thousands of persons each year in early Louisiana. In those days, no one knew that the disease was carried by mosquitoes breeding in stagnant ponds and pools. In 1853, one of the nation's worst outbreaks of yellow fever occurred in New Orleans. At least 7,849 persons died that year, with an average of one death recorded every five minutes by August. About 5 percent of the city's population was stricken.

Dr. Carlos Finlay, a Cuban physician, studied yellow fever in the 1880s and discovered that the disease was carried by the mosquitoes. His findings were confirmed by the U.S. Army's Yellow Fever Commission in 1900, but epidemics continued to sweep Louisiana until 1905. That year, Dr. Quitman Kohnke of New Orleans sponsored an ordinance to screen the cisterns. This simple solution effectively blocked mosquitoes from breeding, and the state has not had a yellow fever problem since. ▪

attempt to take over Cuba, which was still a Spanish colony. Lopez was captured and executed by the Spanish in 1851. William Walker, another filibuster operating out of New Orleans, was tried—but acquitted—for leading similar attacks on Nicaragua in 1857.

The Question of Secession

Louisiana was also caught up in secession fever—whether or not to withdraw from the Union. Like other politicians in the South, Louisiana's leaders believed that state power was more legitimate than that of the federal government. Northern legislators disagreed, and many debates on this issue were held in Congress. The expansion of slavery was another heated issue. Northern states did not want new areas of the country to allow slavery, but Louisiana and its neighbors supported slave ownership. Economic jealousy was an additional factor between the more industrial North and the primarily agricultural South.

The Civil War

Eleven southern states, including Louisiana, finally seceded from the Union on January 26, 1861. Initially, the people of Louisiana were divided. Some people wanted to remain in the Union; others simply thought war was bad for business. At first, Louisiana considered itself a republic and even flew its own flag for six weeks before joining the South—the Confederate States of America. The U.S. Customs House and the Mint were captured in New Orleans, and other federal forts and armories throughout Louisiana were seized and weapons taken. While thousands of Louisianians enlisted, others objected to getting involved in a war simply to protect what they saw as the interests of slaveholders and the upper classes. These independent thinkers, called Jayhawkers, vigorously resisted the Confederacy throughout the war.

It was a year before the fighting caught up with Louisiana. In April 1862, a Union fleet of forty-three ships under Admiral David

The fleets of Admiral Farragut destroying Confederate forts as they sail into New Orleans in 1862

G. Farragut captured New Orleans. After destroying two nearby Confederate forts, Farragut took the city without firing a shot. On May 1, Union troops marched into New Orleans and held it until the end of the war.

Farragut, in the meantime, steamed upriver and captured Baton Rouge and other Louisiana towns along the Mississippi, which meant that the lower Mississippi River was open to commerce throughout the Civil War. Much of inland Louisiana, however, remained in Confederate hands. Opelousas became the state capital in 1863, but the government moved to Shreveport several months later because Union armies were approaching. At war's end, Shreveport was the last holdout of the Confederacy and the last city

"Beast Butler"

During the Civil War (1861–1865), Union troops occupied New Orleans. One Union commander, General Benjamin Butler, issued an infamous order directed at the city's women, who often spat at Union soldiers or refused to serve them in stores and restaurants. Butler said that any woman "insulting a member of the federal forces" in any way would be severely punished— an action that earned him the nickname "Beast Butler." The general left New Orleans at the end of 1862, much to the relief of the city's residents. ■

to fly the flag of the Confederate states. Although the Union never controlled the entire state, the plantation system was in ruins and farms were devastated.

Freedom Granted

The Emancipation Proclamation took effect on January 1, 1863. Although it granted freedom to slaves, slaveholders were allowed

Freedmen voting in New Orleans in 1867

to keep their "property" for a limited time—even in Union-occupied territory. A state constitutional convention in 1864 finally abolished slavery in Louisiana. This constitution remained in effect until 1868, when a "Reconstruction" constitution was approved.

War's Aftermath

After the South lost the war, military governors controlled Louisiana until 1868, when Louisiana was readmitted to the Union and Governor Henry Clay Warmoth and Lieutenant Governor Oscar Dunn were elected. Dunn was the first black person to serve in such a capacity in Louisiana. There was a great deal of corruption, however, in that administration. Taxes soared, and money was stolen from the state treasury. Northerners called "carpetbaggers" came to Louisiana to control affairs behind the scenes. The word *carpetbaggers* is still used to describe outsiders who try to use influence where they are not wanted.

Several white supremacist groups such as the Knights of the White Camellia, the Ku Klux Klan, and the White League wanted to limit the political power of Louisiana's blacks, which was growing after the war. Federal troops were withdrawn in 1877, leav-

After the Civil War, "carpetbaggers" from the North sought to gain powerful positions in Louisiana.

Hard Times

In 1860, Louisiana was considered second in the nation and first in the South for its per-capita wealth. This calculation, however, probably does not include slaves, who made up a large proportion of the population. The slaves were property and their "value" contributed to the white population's wealth. And as a result of the plantation system, a small group of landowners controlled most of the wealth. The damage caused during the Civil War and the political mismanagement that followed, however, knocked Louisiana from its economic perch. In 1880, Louisiana was last in the South and thirty-seventh in the nation in per-capita wealth. ◼

ing the blacks without support. The radical whites tossed out the black politicians, installed their own representatives, and interfered with the right of blacks to vote and hold office. That situation existed until the civil rights movement of the 1960s.

Back on Track

Louisiana had a hard time recovering from the ravages of the Civil War, but some steps were taken to pull the state out of the postwar crisis. The channel at the mouth of the Mississippi was deepened to allow easier passage for freighters, and railroads crisscrossed the state. Levees were rebuilt along the Mississippi River in 1879 to protect towns and farms from flooding. Baton Rouge was named state capital once again in 1882. After the turn of the century, large deposits of natural gas and oil were discovered and sold augmenting the revenue from the sulfur and salt already being mined.

Louisiana was ready to go forward. Progress would be slow, but it was progress.

CHAPTER FOUR

History's Later Chapters

Louisiana changed dramatically after the Civil War. The most obvious changes affected farmworkers, especially in sugar and cotton cultivation. Before the war, plantations used slaves to work the fields. After the war, the big growers had to pay large groups of whites and blacks to harvest cane. Then giant refineries were built in central locations, to be shared by several landowners. Sharecroppers—the small farmers who rented plots of land and worked the cotton fields—had to split their earnings with the landowner to pay their expenses.

Cotton production became an important part of Louisiana's economy after the Civil War.

Many innovations increased productivity and cut labor costs. Duncan Kenner, the founder of the Louisiana Sugar Planters Association, is credited with using movable narrow-gauge railroads to haul cane to the mills. When one field was harvested, the tracks were picked up and carried to the next site.

Railroads and Forests

Railroads altered the face of Louisiana after the Civil War. Between 1880 and 1910, some 5,000 miles (8,047 km) of rail were laid. The trains could then chug into northern and western Louisiana, opening them up to business and development. Towns such as Ruston,

Opposite: Cutting sugarcane

Northern Newcomers

In the 1880s, farmers from the upper Midwest moved to Louisiana to plant wheat. Some had fought for the North in the Civil War, but past anger was put aside, and they usually got along well with the Confederate veterans in Louisiana. ■

Jennings, De Quincy, and De Ridder sprang up where the tracks crossed. Restaurants, hotels, laundries, and other local services were used by the train crews as well as the passengers.

The railroads made lumbering a profitable industry in postwar Louisiana. By 1880, northern lumber companies had cleared the forests of Minnesota, Wisconsin, and Michigan and turned their eyes to the cypress forests of the southern states. The pine woods of northwest, southwest, and eastern Louisiana were also targeted. The timber companies' motto was "Cut Out and Get Out," and they devastated large tracts of land before moving on. After they left, the land was sold to farmers or given to the parishes in lieu of back taxes.

By 1880, timber companies had removed large amounts of cypress from the forests.

Yet Louisianians, both old-timers and new arrivals, rose to this challenge. Around the little town of Independence, hundreds of Italian immigrants snapped up the damaged land at bargain prices. They planted fields of strawberries where there were once stands of trees. Numerous Czech families eagerly settled around Kolin and Libuse and began farming.

Reforested Land

Fields of vegetables and grain eventually covered the damaged landscape. In addition, the state replanted tens of thousands of fast-growing pines and other softwoods to ensure a future supply of trees. Today, Louisiana's Department of Agriculture and Forestry is considered one of the best in the nation for its forest restoration and protection efforts.

With the demise of lumbering, small towns again

Italian and Czech immigrants settled in Louisiana to farm deforested lands.

Pine trees in Kisatchie National Forest

struggled to remain economically viable in an all-too-familiar rerun of Louisiana's boom-or-bust economy. Some communities took many years to recover.

Oil

The emerging oil industry provided the next big economic jump-start. Boomtowns sprang up near newly discovered wells. These were ramshackle communities where fights, gambling, and drunkenness were part of everyday life. Yet some towns, like Trees City, encouraged oil workers to bring their families and settle down. The founders of Trees City—Benedun and Joe Trees—had invented a technique to prevent an oil well from blowing up: pouring concrete into the well and then drilling through the concrete. They wanted their workers to lead productive lives, so they welcomed the wives and children along with the oilmen. Most of these new communities, however, disappeared after the initial oil boom when large companies pushed out the small operators and took over the oil fields.

The construction of pipelines brought some additional economic benefits to Louisiana. Drillers in Texas and Oklahoma needed to get their product to the nearest deepwater port, which was Baton Rouge. Beginning in 1910, long lines of pipes were laid from the oil fields to the city. The oil was then carried south on barges to New Orleans and beyond.

Oil ushered in Louisiana's "age of the automobile." With cars, it was easier to get around the state, and towns began to sprawl out. Commerce expanded as transportation improved.

The Suburbs

Roseland Terrace was Louisiana's first real suburb. Located about 2 miles (3 km) outside Baton Rouge, the planned community was laid out in 1911. At the time, it was considered far outside the city. Soon everyone started buying automobiles, which made commuting easy. ▪

World War I

In 1917, when the United States entered World War I (1914–1918),
thousands of Louisianians joined the military services. The state's
citizens contributed more than $200 million to the Liberty Loan
drive, which helped the government pay its wartime debts.

Good Governors

Governor John M. Parker supported extensive construction of a
paved highway system in 1920. This network of roads enabled
relief supplies to reach the far ends of the state during the Great
Flood of 1927. After record rains, hundreds of square miles of land
were flooded when levees broke and the Mississippi River surged
over the countryside. After the cleanup, numerous water-control
projects were started, with the assistance of the federal government.

**The Great Flood of
1927**

Huey P. Long, governor of Louisiana from 1928 to 1932

Governor Huey P. Long was elected in 1927 and launched the South's most extensive road-building project. His 4.4-mile (7-km) bridge across the Mississippi River in New Orleans, accommodating both railroad and auto traffic, was considered an engineering innovation when it was dedicated in 1935. By 1939, the state had 375,000 registered autos.

Governor Long, nicknamed The Kingfish, was one of America's most colorful political leaders. He served as governor from 1928 to 1932. He became a U.S. senator in 1930 but refused to resign as governor until 1932. As governor, he was a strong advocate of education. Long levied taxes on oil and gas companies to raise money for schools, and free books were distributed to schoolchildren. In addition, he abolished the poll tax, a system that required people to pay in order to vote. Among his other accomplishments, Long built a new state capitol in Baton Rouge and started a school of medicine at Louisiana State University.

The Kingfish Was a Favorite

As senator, Long championed a "Share-the-Wealth" program—a plan designed to distribute the country's wealth to poorer citizens. This program made him a favorite with people who were hungry and out of work, especially because his proposal came at the height of the Great Depression—a worldwide economic crash that closed banks and businesses, forced people off their farms, and shuttered factories. People were desperate for aid, and Long's proposals seemed like the perfect solution.

Long directed a powerful political machine that helped him to get elected to office and to keep his wide-ranging power. Long had many enemies who felt he was a demagogue—someone who tries to stir up the people by emotional appeals in order to achieve power. Just as he was considering a run for the presidency in 1935, Long was assassinated by one of his political opponents.

Long's sudden death ushered in a confusing time for Louisiana politics, especially because O. K. Allen, Long's handpicked successor as governor, also died unexpectedly. Lieutenant Governor James Noe stepped in to fill the term. Richard W. Leche was elected next, but he resigned in a financial scandal in 1939. "Uncle" Earl Long, Leche's lieutenant governor and Huey's brother, served out Leche's term. Earl Long was elected governor in 1948 and 1956. He was another colorful character, noted for throwing wild parties in New Orleans's French Quarter. Earl Long often distributed hams and turkeys to the crowds when he gave speeches, flipping coins to the watching kids. But he and many of his cronies got into trouble with the federal government over frauds involving voting and money. Sam Jones became governor in 1940 as a reform candidate. His efforts to clean up Louisiana succeeded, at least for a time.

World War II

World War II (1939–1945) brought prosperity again. The state's military bases and strong ship-building industry were vital to the U.S. war effort. Its agricultural and industrial products contributed, too. More than 130,000 men and 2,000 women joined the military, and 3,964 died in service.

Social Change

Although the good times continued after the war as income increased, Louisiana still struggled to catch up with the rest of the country. One of the problems continued to be a shaky education

Forced segregation in public places, including prisons, increased social tension in Louisiana after World War II.

system, with an illiteracy rate three times higher than the rest of the country. These were also the bleak days of segregation in many parts of the United States, where blacks and whites were forced to go to separate schools, churches, hospitals, restaurants, and other public places.

The state underwent many social changes between the 1930s and 1960s. After World War II, men who previously worked on farms moved to the cities because they wanted a better life for their families. With the population explosion in the cities, rural Louisiana lost its dominance.

Blacks and Women

The black population of Louisiana still lagged far behind the whites. Kermit A. Parker, a New Orleans pharmacist, decided to run for governor in 1952, becoming the first African-American to

Black Leaders

Attorney Alexander Pierre "A. P." Tureaud (right) was a leader of the fight for racial equality in Louisiana. A descendant of "free people of color," Tureaud devoted his career to handling civil rights issues. From the 1930s through the 1940s, he won cases that contributed to overturning the state's segregation policies. One of his successful suits equalized pay for white and black teachers. Another case led to the desegregation of public schools in New Orleans.

Tureaud was a role model for an entire generation of young African-American activists. One of his law partners, Ernest N. "Dutch" Morial, became the first black in the state legislature since the end of the Civil War. Morial was then elected as two-term mayor of New Orleans (1978–1986), the first black to hold that post. ■

Lucille May Grace, the first woman to run for governor of Louisiana

seek any state office since before the turn of the century. Lucille May Grace, the registrar of the State Land Office, also decided to campaign for governor. She was the first woman to run for this post in Louisiana. Neither Parker nor Grace made it through the primaries, elections in which candidates are chosen by their political parties to run against opponents in other parties. But their efforts opened the way for others of their race and gender to pursue political opportunities. More and more blacks registered to vote, so by the late 1950s, the number of qualified African-Americans in Louisiana was the highest in the South.

Race became Louisiana's most volatile social issue. Centuries of inequality were hard to overcome. Because poor blacks competed for the same jobs as poor whites, there was an additional element of distrust.

Trouble over Schools

Louisiana's segregationist leaders fought hard to preserve segregation in the early 1960s, despite court orders to open up the schools. The crisis escalated in November 1960, when black children attempted to enter several previously all-white schools in New Orleans. Many white parents withdrew their youngsters from the classrooms, and whites and blacks fought in the streets. New Orleans's citizens gradually learned to work together, however, and within a few years, all the city's schools were desegregated.

Leading the way, Governor John J. McKeithen reached out to all races, encouraging them to respect one another. McKeithen also worked hard to bring jobs to the state and won 82 percent of the vote when he ran for reelection in 1967—the greatest margin of victory ever seen in Louisiana.

Bottom Drops Out

In the 1980s, the bottom dropped out of the oil market, and Louisiana was once again gripped by economic crisis. Other challenges faced the state under the administration of Governor Edwin Edwards. Louisiana's public schools were among the worst in the nation, political corruption again was rampant, and population growth had slowed almost to a standstill. Many people left Louisiana, placing additional strains on the state's social services.

In 1987, Governor Charles E. "Buddy" Roemer was elected, defeating Governor Edwards, a longtime Louisiana political leader. Roemer instituted a series of financial "reforms," including a state lottery and riverboat gambling.

Duke vs. Edwards

In 1989, Louisiana was startled when David Duke, a former member of the Ku Klux Klan who had ties to the American Nazi Party and advocated white supremacy, was elected to the state legislature.

Edwin Edwards
campaigning for
governor in 1991

He went on to run as Republican candidate for governor in 1991 against Edwin Edwards, the former governor. Both Democrats and Republicans lambasted Duke for his extremist views, and international media flocked to Louisiana to cover the hard-fought election. Edwards managed to defeat Duke.

Problems Multiply

As the end of the century approached, the state continued to have problems. New Orleans had one of the highest rates of violent crime in the nation. In addition, investigations showed that organized crime had infiltrated the gambling industry. Topping all this, several wealthy, politically connected Louisianians got into legal trouble for cheating the medicare system—a federal government program that helps pay health-care costs. Other well-known state residents were convicted of bribing officials to pass legislation that favored their businesses. Compounding these problems, Louisiana's prisons were overcrowded and police were underpaid.

Despite these challenges, ordinary Louisianians continued to work hard, pay their taxes, and mind their own business. There were many positives. Environmental issues became a priority, and wetlands, bayous, and open spaces were preserved despite pressure from developers. African-Americans and women made great gains in business and politics, and a watchful press kept the spotlight on criminals. Young, open-minded legislators worked to halt the old "business as usual" system. Tourism increased. The population downturn stabilized.

In 1995, Republican Mike Foster was elected governor and promised to support a reform movement. His grandfather, Murphy J. Foster, had been governor at the turn of the century. Between those two centuries and between those two Fosters—Murphy and Mike—Louisiana has come a long way.

CHAPTER FIVE

Louisiana's Low-Lying Land

L ouisiana, the thirty-first largest state, consists of 49,650 square miles (128,593 sq km) of farmland, alligators, street parades, egrets, swamps, music, cypress trees, hot sauce, and colorful characters.

The state's longest north-south distance is 283 miles (455 km), and its widest east-west point is 315 miles (507 km). If you lay a ruler across a map, you can count off about 397 miles (639 km) of coastline along the Gulf. If you include all the bays, inlets, and islands, however, you come up with a coast-line of 7,721 miles (12,426 km).

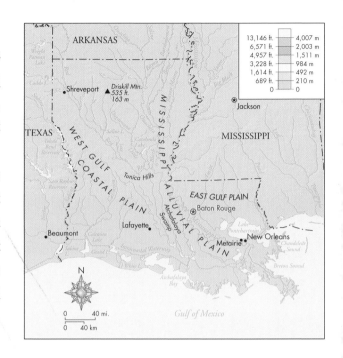

Louisiana's topography

Once Underwater

Millions of years ago, a visitor to what is now Louisiana would have needed to wear high rubber boots to stay dry. Much of the state once lay under the Gulf of Mexico. The land gradually

Lowest Point

The lowest point of the state is 5 feet (1.5 m) below sea level at New Orleans. Levees hold back the waters of the rolling Mississippi, which varies from 30 feet (9.1 m) deep in winter to a spring flood depth of 62 feet (18.9 m) off the French Quarter. This is an interesting twist, because the river itself is 15 feet (5 m) above sea level. Over the centuries, silt from the river piled up along its banks, raising the riverbed higher than the surrounding land. ■

Opposite: Sunrise in Bayou Cocodrie swamp in Atchafalaya Basin

appeared as billions of tons of silt were carried down from the north via the Mississippi and its tributaries.

Land Regions

Louisiana has three main regions. The East Gulf Coastal Plain, which incorporates the land east of the Mississippi and north of Lake Pontchartrain, includes marshes and lowlands. The Mississippi Alluvial Plain lies along the lower Mississippi River from the Arkansas border to the Gulf. The Mississippi River Delta covers 13,000 square miles (33,670 sq km) of rich soil. The bayous, quiet backwaters in the delta, are natural drains for overflow water from the rivers.

Water lilies in the marshlands of Sabine National Wildlife Refuge

The West Gulf Coastal Plain takes in all of Louisiana west of the Mississippi Alluvial Plain. Behind the barrier beaches of the Gulf, marshes stretch inland for up to 20 miles (32 km). Some 2.6 million acres (1 million ha) of marshland along the Louisiana coast accounts for 41 percent of the nation's total. The West Gulf Coastal Plain has an eastern border that runs from Monroe to Alexandria to Lafayette.

Swamp in Moss Bluff (above); Kisatchie Bayou in Kisatchie National Forest (below)

Today, about half of Louisiana's land is forested, much less than a century ago. About one-third of the state consists of wetlands. Prairies once covered more than 15 percent of the state, mostly in the far southwestern part of Louisiana. Smaller patches of prairie

Salt Domes

Louisiana salt domes were created about 150 million years ago, mostly along the Gulf of Mexico. At one time, much of what is now Louisiana was submerged by a shallow salt sea that evaporated after becoming landlocked. Thick layers of salt collected as sediment and were later covered by mud and sand. Geological shifting of the landmass pushed the lighter salt domes and ridges higher. Of the 204 salt domes in the state, 30 are in northern Louisiana and 100 in the coastal region. Oil exploration on the seventy offshore salt domes has yielded excellent results.

Weeks Island is one of the largest domes, towering 160 feet (48 m) above the surrounding marsh. Avery Island is 155 feet (47 m) high and covers 2,500 acres (1,012 ha).

The Five Islands—Avery (above), Weeks, Jefferson, Cote Blanche, and Bell—have been heavily mined over the past century. Only Weeks, Avery, and Cote Blanche are still active, but it will be a long time before Louisiana's salt runs out. ▨

Louisiana's Geographical Features

Total area; rank	49,650 sq. mi. (128,593 sq km); 31st
Land; rank	43,566 sq. mi. (112,835 sq km); 33rd
Water; rank	6,084 sq. mi. (15,757 sq km); 6th
Inland water; **rank**	4,153 sq. mi. (10,756 sq km); 5th
Coastal water; **rank**	1,931 sq. mi. (5,001 sq km); 3rd
Geographic center	Avoyelles, 3 miles (5 km) southeast of Marksville
Highest point	Driskill Mountain, 535 feet (163 m)
Lowest point	–5 feet (–1.5 m) at New Orleans
Largest city	New Orleans
Longest river	Mississippi River, 305 miles (491 km) in Louisiana out of a total length of 2,340 miles (3,766 km)
Population; rank	4,238,21 (1990 census); 21st
Record high temperature	114°F (46°C) at Plain Dealing on August 10, 1936
Record low temperature	–16°F (–27°C) at Minden on February 13, 1899
Average July temperature	82°F (28°C)
Average January temperature	50°F (10°C)
Average annual precipitation	57 inches (145 cm)

land covered areas drained by the Ouachita River and parts of the northern parishes. Today, most of that prairie land is gone, except for a 60-mile (96-km) strip north of the Gulf Coast marsh that stretches to Texas. Gone also are the prairie chickens, prairie voles, Mississippi kites, and other animals that once lived there. The prairie was plowed for farmland or converted for pasture by the end of the nineteenth century.

Another interesting landscape form in Louisiana is the *chênière,* which is a French word meaning "place where oaks grow." Chênières are found only in Cameron and Vermillion Parishes near the Gulf of Mexico. Local residents called them "islands in the marsh." They are formed by the Mississippi River, which dumped clay and sand as it shifted its path. When the river changed direction, shell fragments and other debris from the sea were added to the clay piles, which were sometimes as high as 2 to 10 feet (0.6 to 3 m) high, 10 to 50 miles (16 to 80 km) long, and .25 miles (400 m) wide. Eventually, the river would shift again, creating acres of marshland where there was once beach.

Yes, There Is a Mountain

At 535 feet (163 m), Driskill Mountain is the highest point in the state. That might not seem impressive, but Driskill is higher than the highest points in Florida and Delaware, and Louisianians are proud of it. This tree-shrouded mountain in north-central Louisiana is a favorite of hikers and campers.

Driskill Mountain is part of Nacogodches Wold, a high, treeless plain. Millions of years ago, the Earth's crust was pushed up in a great geological movement that raised a dome of rock skyward. Erosion over the centuries wore the rock down to its present height.

Rolling hills cover most of south-central and eastern Louisiana, especially in West Feliciana Parish. The Tunica Hills in central-eastern Louisiana have deep, rich soil that is good for cotton farming. Beef cattle now graze in pastures that were once plantations. Some land has reverted to forests of beech, oak, and fragrant magnolia.

The soil here, called *loess* (LESS), resulted from glaciers grinding up the landscape in the far north millions of years ago. The

Cotton plants thrive in the rich soil of Louisiana.

Mississippi River floods then carried this sediment south, depositing it as fertile farmland after the water receded. Sometimes, these walls of silt are 35 feet (11 m) deep.

Waterways

In addition to its rivers—the Mississippi, Black, Ouachita, Pearl, Sabine, Red, Calcasieu—and other waterways, Louisiana has 4,153 square miles (10,756 sq km) of inland lakes. The state's largest body of water is the salty, shallow Lake Pontchartrain, which sprawls across 625 square miles (1,619 sq km) north of New Orleans.

A major water attraction is the Toledo Bend Reservoir, which Louisiana shares with Texas. The reservoir, which covers 284 square miles (735 sq km), is the fourth-largest man-made lake in

A Long Race

To promote a boat race at the Celtic Nations Festival in New Orleans, Danny O'Flaherty, a local bar owner and musician, rowed across Lake Pontchartrain in September 1997.

He left New Orleans at 5 A.M., aiming for the Madisonville Wooden Boat Festival on the opposite shore. Battling 4-foot (1.2-m) waves, he made it across 31 miles (50 km) in 9 hours and 40 minutes.

O'Flaherty rowed a skinny 22-foot (7-m) long currach (KUH-ruh). This is a canoelike boat similar to the one his father used off the coast of Ireland. ■

The Mississippi is the most important of Louisiana's many rivers.

the United States. It supplies municipal, industrial, and irrigation water to the Sabine River Basin. The lake was made by damming the Sabine River in 1966. The Atchafalaya River Basin, Louisiana's best-known swamp, is sandwiched between two levees built about 18 miles (29 km) apart. The Mississippi River meanders for

120 miles (193 km) through the heart of this magnificent wetland, from the Old River Control Structure to Atchafalaya Bay.

Rivers and Wetlands

Atchafalaya means "long river" in the language of the Atakapa people who once lived in the region, and the name is appropriate. The flowage is more than 1.3 billion gallons (4.9 billion l) of water every day, carrying tons of muddy sediment from the north. The soil buildup has changed the look of the Atchafalaya over the past sixty years. Islands are built up, lakes filled, and the river channel twists and turns in new directions, providing an ever-changing landscape.

Conservation efforts in various parts of the state have saved some wetlands and marshes. For example, to rescue a dying marsh at Caernarvon south of New Orleans, fresh water from the Mississippi was diverted into an area almost killed by salt-water intrusion. Today, willows bloom, ducks land, and fish have returned. The diversion, however, has caused another challenge—oystermen say that the fresh water is destroying their oyster beds. There is also the possibility that pollution from the river caused a disease that wiped out

Saving the Streams

The Louisiana Natural and Scenic Streams System includes forty-nine protected waterways. They are beautiful wildlife habitats and recreation areas for hikers and canoeists. Laws were passed in 1970 to save these streams and rivers from channeling, straightening, and development. ■

Because of successful conservation efforts, wildlife, such as these opposums, have returned to the wetlands and marshes.

many of the oyster beds in the early 1990s. Environmentalists hope to find a balance between the needs of nature and those of people.

Louisiana's Woodlands

Of the 10 million acres (4 million ha) of forest in northern Louisiana, more than 90 percent is privately owned and planted with pines. This leaves only 300,000 acres (121,406 ha) of state wildlife-management areas and 700,000 acres (283,280 ha) of federal lands for nature's diversity. Many botanists and other plant scientists are concerned that an attack of the southern pine beetle or another pest could wipe out an entire forest.

The 600,000-acre (242,812-ha) Kisatchie Forest is the state's only national forest. Kisatchie's six districts sprawl over central and northern

Louisiana in a vast carpet of green. Some of its waterways are home to rare mussels, a form of shellfish. Longleaf pine trees here were once 5 feet (1.5 m) across and more than 100 feet (30 m) high, but loggers cut down the Louisiana forests from the turn of the century through the 1930s. This process, called clear-cutting, means that the state's forests today are mostly second-growth trees.

In addition, many stands of trees were cut down in the early 1970s when the price of soybeans rose to more than $10 a bushel.

A small lake in central Louisiana near Kisatchie National Forest

Opposite: A great egret at her nest in Atchafalaya Basin

Louisiana's parks and forests map

ARKANSAS

TEXAS

MISSISSIPPI

KISATCHIE NATIONAL FOREST

KISATCHIE NATIONAL FOREST

KISATCHIE NATIONAL FOREST

Shreveport

North Toledo Bend

Beaumont

Lafayette

Baton Rouge

Metairie   New Orleans

Jackson

N

0   40 mi.

0   40 km

Gulf of Mexico

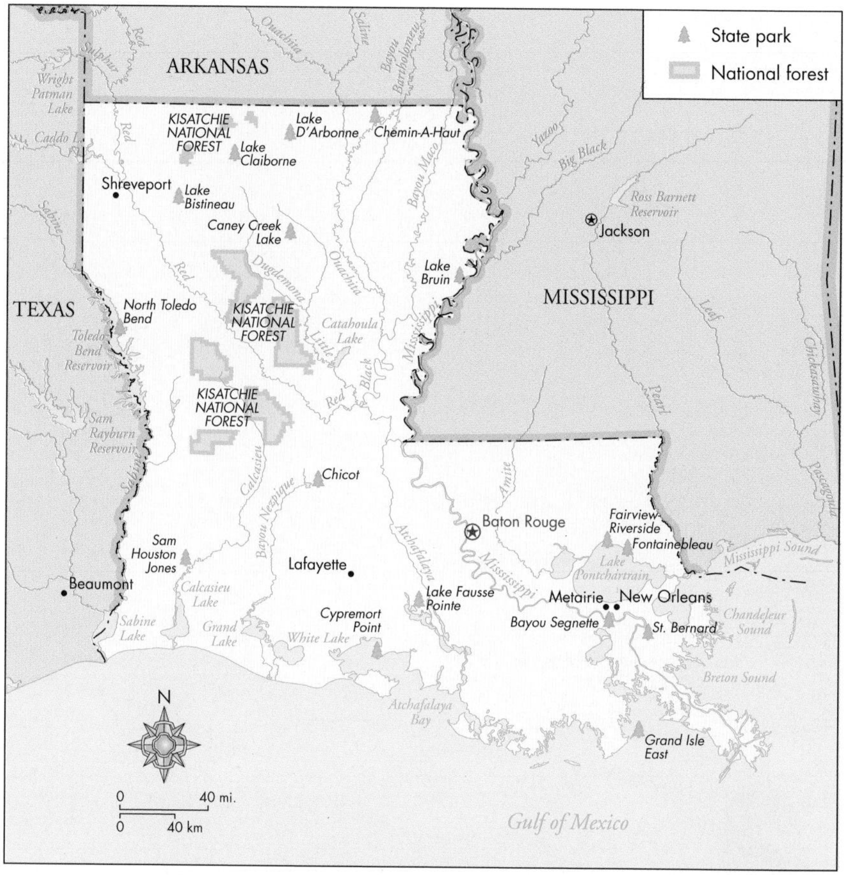

Clear-Cutting

More than 4 million acres (1.6 million ha) of timber were cleared during the peak years of lumbering between 1904 and 1927. The owners of these companies did not live in Louisiana and cared little what happened to the landscape as long as they made money. ■

Farmers and corporations cleared thousands of acres of land and planted soybeans to meet the worldwide demand. Within a few years, the oversupply of beans drove down the prices. The farmers went bankrupt, but it was too late to save the trees. In addition, the landscape has been damaged by floods that wash away soil once protected by tree roots.

Since the late 1970s, however, massive reforestation efforts have been successful in some parts of Louisiana, such as the Kisatchie National Forest. Second-growth trees are fast-growing pines up to 90 feet (27 m) tall. By the 1990s, more trees were being planted than were being cut.

State Parks

Louisiana now has thirty-one state parks, commemorative areas, and state preservation areas to safeguard its natural beauty. These protected areas make the state a garden of wild azalea, pink orchid, candy root, yellow pitcher plant, blackberries, and mayhaw. The park system includes St. Bernard State Park along the Mississippi River, only 19 miles (30 km) from downtown New Orleans. The Louisiana State Arboretum near Ville Platte features a lush beech-magnolia forest and 150 species of plants.

Dogwood blossom in a protected national park

Louisiana Wildlife

All sorts of animals—from the great to the small—call Louisiana their home. Among the tiniest are short-tailed shrews that weigh less than 1/3 ounce (9 grams). Then there are toads, red crawfish, and twenty-two species of salamanders. The Texas rat snake can swallow duck eggs twice the size of its head, thanks to the hinge in its lower jaw. Domestic pigs—turned loose and now feral (wild)—often have large tusks and eat almost anything. Herds of these foraging pigs can cause a lot of damage. As they snuffle along, they dig up roots, munch on leaves, and topple saplings.

Louisiana hosts more migrating blackbirds, grackles, and related species than any other state. Bald eagles winter on Cross and Caddo Lakes as well as at Toledo Bend, and feed on the fish found in the murky waters. An estimated 15 million blackbirds roost around Miller Lake. Egrets, cormorants, herons, coots, falcons, woodpeckers, and ducks are among the many other varieties of birds. The brown pelican, the state bird, gives Louisiana its nickname: the Pelican State.

The Weather

Louisiana's climate is semitropical in the south and moderate in the north. The record high temperature of 114°F (46°C) was set at Plain Dealing on August 10, 1936. The coldest temperature was –16°F (–27°C) at Minden on February 13, 1899. Louisiana's weather is consistent—muggy in the summer and cool in the winter. The average July temperature is 82°F (28°C), and the average January temperature is 50°F (10°C). The state gets a lot of rain, usually around 57 inches (145 cm) a year.

Bald eagles hunt for fish in Louisiana's freshwater lakes.

Sometimes, however, Louisiana's weather can be tricky. Hurricane Audrey was one of the worst storms ever to hit the Louisiana coast. Originating in the Gulf of Yucatán in July 1957, the storm gained strength as it headed northward. Warnings came almost too late to be of any help.

As Audrey approached land, it was preceded by a 30-foot (9-m) tidal wave that washed over the levees. Between 400 and 500 people died, and property damage amounted to $150 million. Yet even that fierce storm wasn't as deadly as the hurricane that had smashed ashore in 1893 at Chenitre Caminada, killing 1,800 persons.

Roseate spoonbills fighting for nest area on Rabbit Island

CHAPTER SIX

Louisiana's Ethereal Cities

Each area of Louisiana has its own special flavor, thanks to its history and its people. Let's take a stroll through the state and learn more.

Northeastern Louisiana was settled by tough Protestant Scots and Scotch-Irish pioneers. Later, Germans traveled westward from Mississippi, Tennessee, and Kentucky and the more-settled Eastern Seaboard colonies. The Native Americans who first lived here called this area *Ouachita* (WAH-suh-taw), which means "Land of the Sacred Silver Waters." Cotton was the economic backbone of the region before the Civil War.

Monroe is the largest city in the northeast. The Emy-Lou Biedenharn Bible Research Museum is one of the most interesting attractions, housing antique Bibles and musical instruments. The museum has a 700-pound (318-kg) front door that is specially hinged for easy opening. Joseph Biedenharn, the first bottler of Coca-Cola, lived here in the early twentieth century.

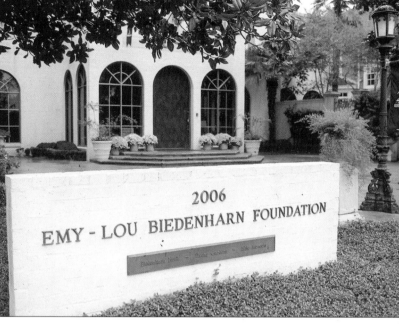

The Emy-Lou Biedenharn Bible Research Museum in Monroe

Sports Paradise

This part of Louisiana is a sports lovers' paradise with numerous wildlife-management areas, trails, bird sanctuaries, and recreational facilities. One of the best known is the D'Arbonne National Wildlife

Opposite: New Orleans skyline and Mississippi River at dusk

Shreveport, the second-largest city in Louisiana

Refuge at Farmerville north of Monroe, a habitat for alligators and numerous bird species. Now let's turn our attention to northwest Louisiana, split by the muddy waters of the Red River.

The largest city in the northwest is the industrial community of Shreveport, named after Captain Henry Shreve. Shreve became famous for breaking up a 160-mile (257-km) logjam on the Red River in 1832. In five years, he had cleared a narrow passage, but it took another forty years to open the river completely.

Moving southward to the heart of Louisiana, Alexandria and Pineville proudly claim to be the crossroads of the state. Trading posts were established there as early as 1723. Missionaries and gamblers, cattlemen and soldiers, came through this area from Mississippi, heading for the Texas frontier or the bright lights of New Orleans.

Nickname Earned

State capital Baton Rouge earned its name when French explorer André Pénicaut spotted a red stick on the bluffs above the Mississippi River in 1700. The *baton rouge* (red stick) marked the boundaries between the Bayou Goula and Houma hunting grounds. In 1719, the

Natchitoches

Founded in 1714, Natchitoches (NAK-uh-tosh) is the oldest settlement in Louisiana. Several Indian tribes lived there when Spanish explorer de Soto arrived in 1542. ■

Old state capitol (left) in Baton Rouge

The law school of Louisiana State University, Baton Rouge

French established a fort on the site, and the city has been one of the state's leading communities ever since.

Because of its location, Baton Rouge was always a military garrison. The French, Spanish, and British had forts in the area. The Pentagon Barracks were built in 1819 to house troops. Many famous Americans served in the fort, including the future president Zachary Taylor and the future Confederate general Robert E. Lee. The city has many other

well-known attractions, such as a Firefighters' Museum, Louisiana State University, and Catfish Town—a restored warehouse district.

When outsiders think of Louisiana, they often think of Cajuns, the descendants of the French Canadian natives expelled from Nova Scotia, then known as Acadia, by the British in the eighteenth-century. Many refugees eventually made their way to French-speaking Louisiana and settled in the bayou country.

Cajun Lifestyle

"Cajun" is a lifestyle that encompasses many cultures. There are hints of a different feeling in the air well before reaching the obvious Cajun parishes of St. Landry, Evangeline, and Acadia.

This transition can be seen as early as Bunkie, in Avoyelles Parish, 120 miles (193 km) northwest of New Orleans, where the leafy old oaks lining the backroads still hint at plantation life.

The Capitol

New Orleans was Louisiana's capital under the French and Spanish, but the state's constitutional convention in 1845 decreed that the site had to be moved more than 60 miles (96 km) from the city to accommodate northern Louisianians. Baton Rouge was selected for its central location and port facilities.

Construction of the new castlelike capitol, complete with gaslight, was completed in 1849. Confederate prisoners were held there during the Civil War until the building was damaged by fire in 1862. The new capitol (left), completed in 1932, is one of the tallest public buildings in the country. Towering thirty-four stories high, it can legitimately claim to be the nation's tallest state capitol. ■

A Cajun musician plays traditional music at Festivals Acadiens in Lafayette.

Ville Platte, some 28 miles (45 km) south of Bunkie, was founded by British and French immigrants, not by Acadian refugees. The locals tend to emphasize that Marcellin Garand, the town's first mayor, was once an officer in Napoleon's army.

Prairie Capital

Going deeper into Cajun country, the town of Eunice calls itself the Capital of the Cajun Prairie. In addition to its strong loyalty to anything Cajun, Eunice sponsors the World Championship Crawfish Etoufée Cook-off

Steaming-hot boiled crawfish

Visitor at the annual New Orleans Jazz & Heritage Festival, enjoying a Cajun specialty

each March. Amateur and professional cooks compete for prizes, and visitors can taste the winning dishes.

Opelousas

The next stop on a ride through Louisiana is Opelousas, whose favorite son is frontiersman Jim Bowie. Bowie invented the wicked-looking knife named after him. He was born in Tennessee, but his family moved to Opelousas when he was only seven years old. Their family plantation, which once encompassed 20,000 acres (8,100 ha) has been carved up into industrial tracts and housing developments. The original family estate is now the site of the Jim Bowie Branch of the First National Bank. Bowie moved to Texas in 1827, where he died in the Battle of the Alamo.

Opelousas is an Indian word meaning either "black leg" or "salt water," but the town is decidedly French. Local farmers help one another to build barns and other houses in a custom called *coup de main.* Some people say the town is so French that the dogs don't understand English.

Old Plantations

The next towns on your tour are Washington and Grand Coteau, where there are several plantations and historical buildings. Magnolia Ridge, a beautiful house built in 1830, and the graceful Academy of the Sacred Heart, built in 1821, are two fine examples of pre–Civil War architecture.

From there, you move on to Lafayette, which proudly proclaims itself as the heart of Cajun Country. In the eighteenth cen-

Rosedown Plantation and its historic gardens, built in St. Francisville in 1835

tury, it was a sleepy village called Petit Manchac. Today, Lafayette is a bustling city with shopping malls.

A statue of Confederate general Alfred Mouton stands at the corner of Jefferson and Lee Streets in Lafayette, keeping an eye on the oilmen who flock to the city to make deals. In addition to the oil business, the town is home to Acadian Village—a re-creation of a typical Acadian town of the early nineteenth century.

The Live Oak Society

The Live Oak Society was founded in Lafayette by Dr. Edwin L. Stephens, first president of the University of Southwestern Louisiana. "Members" of the society are 100-year-olds— oak trees, that is. If a tree's age cannot be proved, it can still be a member of the society if it measures at least 17 feet (5 m) around.

Each member tree has a guardian—a person who traces its history and works for its preservation. Each member tree also pays annual "dues" of twenty-five acorns. The acorns are then planted in a nursery to ensure that there will be a good supply of oak seedlings for the future. ■

Interior of a recreated nineteenth-century building in Acadian Village

The Evangeline Oak site in St. Martinville commemorates the Acadian exile from Nova Scotia in 1755.

Cajun History Recreated

Several historic houses were moved to Acadian Village from other areas. Costumed interpreters, flocks of chickens and guinea hens, and regular old-time Cajun dances make the Acadian Village a lively place.

St. Martinville became the new home of the fictional Evangeline, one of the best known of the Acadian refugees. Poet Henry Wadsworth Longfellow wrote his famous story about a young girl and her sweetheart who were separated for years after the dispersal of the Acadian people. The story is based on the true tale of two young people who were separated on the trip from Canada and met each other again in St. Martinville. Although Wadsworth never visited Louisiana, he captured the emotions of that time.

The Longfellow-Evangeline State Commemorative Area, a 157-acre (63-ha) park, lies along the Bayou Teche (TESH). A museum there tells of the Acadians' arrival in the area and how they became a part of the existing French community. The park was once a *vacherie* (cattle ranch).

Come to Eat

New Iberia is the place where everyone comes to eat. About

New Iberia

New Iberia was first settled by French colonists under Spanish rule. They were then followed by people from the Canary Islands— small pinpoints of land off the coast of western Africa. The settlers grew flax before switching to cattleranching. ■

40 miles (64 km) south of Lafayette, the city's numerous restaurants offer mouth-watering stuffed crabs, bread pudding in rum sauce, baked or broiled flounder, and many other delectable Louisiana dishes.

Farmers around New Iberia grow tons of rice each year, much of which is processed at the Konriko Rice Mill south of town, which offers tours for visitors. The city is also home to sugarcane refineries. Some of the prettiest plantation houses in the South today are found here. Shadows-on-the-Teche, built in 1834, is one of the most famous. Its stately pillars and moss-draped trees add a dreamlike effect, especially on misty mornings.

Evangeline

A statue of Evangeline—the young woman in Henry Wadsworth Longfellow's poem—sits near a small graveyard behind St. Martin of Tours Church in St. Martinville. The statue is modeled after actress Dolores del Rio, who starred in the movie *Evangeline* (1929). ■

Shadows-on-the-Teche Plantation in New Iberia, built in 1834

Hot Sauce on Avery Island

Tabasco, a fiery hot sauce, is made on Avery Island, a land-locked salt dome 7 miles (11 km) south of New Iberia. The plant is located within a sanctuary for snowy egrets and surrounded by a large flower garden. The island is owned by the McIlhenny family, descendants of John Hays, who discovered salt springs there in the late eighteenth century.

Edmund McIlhenny, a New Orleans banker, married Mary Avery in the 1860s and moved to Avery Island when he retired. He liked to play around with recipes and came up with Tabasco sauce in 1868. His first batch amounted to 350 bottles.

Today, more than 60 million bottles of Tabasco are produced each year from the original formula. ◼

Southwest Louisiana

Southwest Louisiana has just about everything in its landscape, including prairies, bayous, and beaches. Its remoteness once made it a perfect haven for pirates. Pecan Island supposedly holds a treasure of gold hidden by pirate Jean Lafitte and his men. Today, oil rigs dot the offshore waters, and rice plantations stretch

An oil platform off Louisiana's shore

for miles. The Gulf Intracoastal Waterway, which divides the region, is an artificial waterway—a 14,300-mile (23,014-km) shipping canal that links Texas to Florida. In Louisiana, the Mississippi River, along with the state's other rivers and waterways, gives Louisiana approximately 2,500 miles (4,025 km) of navigable water.

Contraband Days Celebrated

People here still like to celebrate the good old days. In April, Lake Charles hosts its Contraband Days in honor of long-dead pirates, such as Jean Lafitte, who hid out in nearby marshes. Interstate 10, which runs east to west through the city, parallels the old Spanish Trail. Cattlemen used this route to move their herds between Texas and Louisiana. Today, you see oil company headquarters instead of cattle.

Interesting Spots

Among the many interesting communities is the town of Sulphur, built in 1913 to feed and house the miners who came to work in a nearby sulfur dome. The Brimstone Museum in Sulphur contains many displays highlighting the volatile yellow mineral.

Fort Polk, near Leesville, was established in 1941. The fort was named after Episcopal priest Leonidas Polk, who fought for the Confederacy during the Civil War. Famous officers based there over the years include General George Patton and President Dwight D. Eisenhower. Fort Polk's resident battalions subsequently served in the Gulf War, Somalia, and Bosnia. From this part of Louisiana, all roads lead to Texas, the state's western neighbor.

To the south, more bayou country leads to the Mississippi River. Although there are several free ferry crossings, a bridge between Baton Rouge and New Orleans was built over the river at Donaldsonville. The Sunshine Bridge was constructed during the 1960–1964 administration of Governor Jimmie Davis. Because the governor's favorite song was "You Are My Sunshine," it seemed like the perfect name.

Visit the Big Easy

Of all Louisiana cities, New Orleans is probably the best known. It has numerous nicknames: the Big Easy, for its wild nightlife; the Crescent City, because it sits on a great bend of the Mississippi River; and NOLA, the shortened form of New Orleans, Louisiana. But whatever you call New Orleans, it is one of the most diverse communities in the United States.

New Orleans and the Mississippi

New Orleans owes its existence to economics. The city is strategically located 110 miles (177 km) north of the Gulf of Mexico, where the shifting sandbars and the everchanging Mississippi River Channel are not a problem. René-Robert Cavelier, Sieur de La Salle, explored Louisiana in the late 1680s in the name of King Louis XIV of France. It was not until 1718 that Jean-Baptiste Le Moyne, Sieur de Bienville, established a French outpost there and named it New Orleans after Philippe II, Duc d'Orléans.

From these humble beginnings amid the mosquitoes, alligators, and swamps, a modern city grew and flourished. New Orleans has survived attack by the British during the War of 1812, epidemics of cholera and yellow fever, damage by fire and hurricanes, and occupation by Union troops in the Civil War.

The historic French Quarter—filled with shops, restaurants, and music—is one of the city's most popular centers.

The city's French Quarter, also called the *Vieux Carré* (Old Square), is one of its most popular districts. The French Quarter is noted for its nightclubs and souvenir shops, its restaurants, and its music. Actually, the atmosphere is more Italian than French because thousands of Sicilian immigrants settled here over the past century. Today, a new group of people call the French Quarter home. Many buildings are now owned by East Indians. But Jackson Square and the French Market remain the heart of New Orleans. In the square, a statue of General Andrew Jackson and his horse fronts buildings erected by Spanish colonizers. A block away, the Mississippi River rolls along, prevented from overwhelming the city by a series of levees—high walls made of earth and concrete.

No one can be bored in New Orleans. There are plenty of things to see and do. The Amistad Center at Tulane University houses one of the country's largest collections of facts and artifacts related to African-American heritage. The Louisiana State Museum is part of the former U.S. Mint, which now displays Mardi Gras costumes and an extensive collection of jazz material. Not far away, Preservation Hall, the mecca of traditional jazz, has open seating on folding chairs, but nobody minds. The greatest names in music perform there.

The Marsh

New Orleans's neighborhoods were built on any available dry land. The natural bedrock under the city is more than 70 feet (21 m) beneath the mud, sand, and silt. The marshy ground on which the city sits is settling at an average rate of 3 inches (8 cm) per century. Residents joke that Mardi Gras may someday be a parade of sailboats. ■

Other New Orleans attractions include the American Italian Heritage Museum; O'Flaherty's Irish Channel Pub; City Park; the historic Garden District; the Voodoo Museum; Orpheum Theater; Mary, Queen of Vietnam, Catholic Church; Deutsches Haus German cultural center; New Orleans Aquarium; and the Kosher Cajun Deli & Grocery.

Toss in the Mardi Gras, the steamboats, and the neighborhood festivals—they are all part of the wonderful jambalaya of New Orleans.

New Orleans is known for its long jazz tradition, and street musicians perform throughout the city.

CHAPTER SEVEN

Politics in the Pelican State

ouisiana's governmental structure consists of three branches: executive, legislative, and judicial.

The executive branch of government includes the governor, lieutenant governor, secretary of state, attorney general, state treasurer, and the commissioners of agriculture, insurance, and elections. These elected officials serve four-year terms.

The First Governor

The first territorial governor of Louisiana was William Charles Cole ("C. C.") Claiborne. He was responsible for military, judicial, and civil authority in Louisiana. On December 30, 1803, drums rattled and bugles blared at the Place d'Armes, the central square in New Orleans, as Claiborne relieved the French authorities of their responsibilities in Louisiana.

Claiborne faced many challenges as the U.S. representative in the Louisiana Territory. The Creoles disliked him because he was unfamiliar with their culture and could not speak French. Border disputes with Spain were unsettling, as was the threat of an attack by some disgruntled Americans led by Aaron Burr. These men wanted to form a separate country, independent of the United States, Mexico, or Spain. Burr and his men were arrested, however, ending the possible rebellion.

William C. C. Claiborne, governor of Louisiana Territory and, later, of the state of Louisiana

Opposite: The steps of the capitol in Baton Rouge are inscribed with the names of the states.

Louisiana's Governors

Name	Party	Term	Name	Party	Term
Stevens T. Mason	Dem.	1837–1840	Murphy J. Foster	Dem.	1892–1900
W. C. C. Claiborne	Jeff. Rep.*	1812–1816	William W. Heard	Dem.	1900–1904
Jacques Villere	Jeff. Rep.*	1816–1820	Newton C. Blanchard	Dem.	1904–1908
Thomas B. Robertson	Jeff. Rep.*	1820–1824	Jared Y. Sanders	Dem.	1908–1912
Henry S. Thibodaux	Jeff. Rep.*	1824	Luther E. Hall	Dem.	1912–1916
Henry Johnson	Jeff. Rep.*	1824–1828	Ruffin G. Pleasant	Dem.	1916–1920
Pierre Derbigny	Jeff. Rep.*	1828–1829	John M. Parker	Dem.	1920–1924
Armand Beauvais	Jeff. Rep.*	1829–1830	Henry L. Fuqua	Dem.	1924–1926
Jacques Dupré	Jeff. Rep.*	1830–1831	Oramel H. Simpson	Dem.	1926–1928
André B. Roman	Whig	1831–1835	Huey P. Long	Dem.	1928–1932
Edward D. White	Whig	1835–1839	Alvin O. King	Dem.	1932
André B. Roman	Whig	1839–1843	Oscar K. Allen	Dem.	1932–1936
Alexandre Mouton	Dem.	1843–1846	James A. Noe	Dem.	1936
Isaac Johnson	Dem.	1846–1850	Richard W. Leche	Dem.	1936–1939
Joseph Walker	Dem.	1850–1853	Earl K. Long	Dem.	1939–1940
Paul O. Hebert	Dem.	1853–1856	Sam H. Jones	Dem.	1940–1944
Robert C. Wickliffe	Dem.	1856–1860	Jimmie H. Davis	Dem.	1944–1948
Thomas O. Moore	Dem.	1860–1862	Earl K. Long	Dem.	1948–1952
Federal Military Rule		1862–1864	Robert F. Kennon	Dem.	1952–1956
Henry W. Allen	Dem.	1864–1865	Earl K. Long	Dem.	1956–1960
Michael Hahn	Rep.	1864–1865	Jimmie H. Davis	Dem.	1960–1964
James M. Wells	Rep.	1865–1867	John J. McKeithen	Dem.	1964–1972
Benjamin Flanders	Rep.	1867–1868	Edwin W. Edwards	Dem.	1972–1980
Joshua Baker	Rep.	1868	David C. Treen	Rep.	1980–1984
Henry C. Warmoth	Rep.	1868–1872	Edwin W. Edwards	Dem.	1984–1988
P. B. S. Pinchback	Rep.	1872–1873	Buddy Roemer	Rep.†	1988–1992
John McEnery	Dem.	1873	Edwin W. Edwards	Dem.	1992–1996
William P. Kellogg	Rep.	1873–1877	Murphy J. (Mike)		
Francis T. Nicholls	Dem.	1877–1880	Foster Jr.	Rep.	1996–
Louis A. Wiltz	Dem.	1880–1881			
Samuel D. McEnery	Dem.	1881–1888	*Jeffersonian Republican		
Francis T. Nicholls	Dem.	1888–1892	† Elected a Democrat, switched to Republican		

First Women in Congress

Louisiana's first elected woman senator was Mary Landrieu, a Democrat born in Baton Rouge in 1955 and daughter of Moon Landrieu, a former mayor of New Orleans.

Landrieu (right) served as a Louisiana state representative from 1979 to 1987 and state treasurer from 1987 to 1995. She tried to win the nomination for governor but was defeated in the primaries in 1996. She then went on to run for the U.S. Senate and was elected.

A popular political leader in the Pelican State, Landrieu earned national recognition for supporting social causes and women's issues. She is considered one of the country's leading Democratic women.

Lindy Boggs was Louisiana's first woman U.S. representative. She was elected in 1973. ■

West Florida Rebels

When residents of the "Florida Parishes" in eastern Louisiana rose up against Spain in 1810, President James Madison ordered Governor Claiborne to take possession of the former Spanish colony of West Florida, which was adjacent to Louisiana. The governor's successful action extended American power along the entire Gulf Coast.

Escaped from Troops

Few modern governors have had as much power as Claiborne. Most never have been required to declare war or defend borders. During the Civil War, however, Louisiana's resourceful Confederate governors Thomas O. Moore and Henry W. Allen had to rely on their wits as they scrambled from town to town ahead of advancing Union troops to escape capture and imprisonment by the Union troops.

Duties of the Governor

The governor now has the power to approve or veto any bill passed by the legislature. But there is a safety net—the legislature can then override the governor's veto by a two-thirds' vote in each house. If the governor is unable to perform the tasks of office, the lieutenant governor steps in. Among other important duties, the lieutenant governor also serves as commissioner of the Department of Culture, Recreation and Tourism.

The Constitution

Louisiana adopted a new constitution in 1845. The provision that only landowners could vote was dropped, and election of the governor by direct popular vote was approved. Except for the 1868 constitution, the state's seven other constitutions were based on the 1845 document. ■

The Legislative Branch

As a territory, Louisiana had a house of representatives and a legislative council. The president of the United States appointed the legislative council for five-year terms.

Today, the legislative branch consists of a 39-member Senate and a 105-member House of Representatives. Members of both houses are elected for four-year terms. The Louisiana legislature convenes annually. In odd-numbered years, the speaker of the house opens the legislative session at noon on the last Monday in March. In even-numbered years, the session opens at noon on the last Monday in April.

The Courts

Louisiana has a state supreme court, courts of appeal, district courts, and other lesser courts. The supreme court has a chief justice and six associate justices, all elected for ten-year terms. The associate justice with the longest tenure on the court is named the chief justice. The Louisiana court system has five courts of appeal and forty district courts that handle criminal cases. Some courts deal with special cases in their own backyard. For instance, the Fifteenth Judicial District Court in coastal Louisiana hears cases involving disputes over oil drilling. These cases can involve intricate financial deals or industry-related injuries and property damage. About 10,000 civil cases and 7,500 criminal cases are filed each year in the fifteenth district.

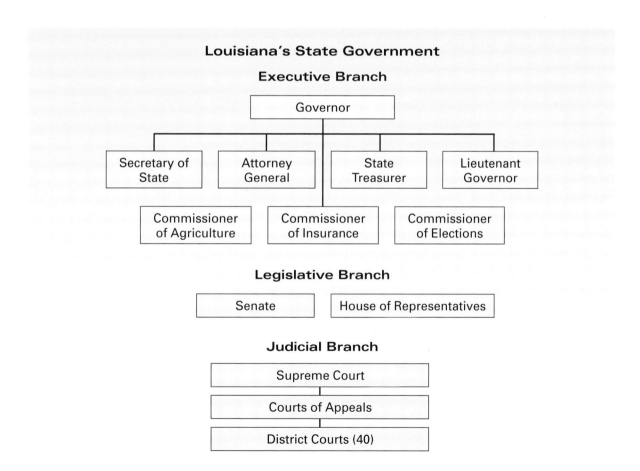

Louisiana's State Government

Executive Branch

Governor

Secretary of State | Attorney General | State Treasurer | Lieutenant Governor

Commissioner of Agriculture | Commissioner of Insurance | Commissioner of Elections

Legislative Branch

Senate | House of Representatives

Judicial Branch

Supreme Court

Courts of Appeals

District Courts (40)

Louisiana's court system is different from those of other states. Louisiana follows the Code Napoléon, rather than English common law. Under the common law system, a judicial decision depends on previous court decisions and on the citizens' customs. Louisiana's judges, on the other hand, decide cases on a strict set of rules—a code of law—and are not required to follow precedents set in previous cases.

Louisiana's Flags

Louisiana has had more official flags than almost any other state in the Union.

The first was the Spanish royal flag of 1519, used by explorer Alonso Alvarez de Pineda when he led an expedition along the shores of the Gulf of Mexico. Next was the French flag, flown by Sieur de la Salle in 1682 when he took possession of Louisiana in the name of Louis XIV of France.

Another Spanish flag flew over the colony in 1762 after parts of Louisiana were ceded to Spain in a transaction between Louis XV and King Charles III of Spain. Then came the English. In the Treaty of Paris that ended the French and Indian War in 1763, England acquired parts of Louisiana east of the Mississippi River from France and Spain.

Louisiana reverted to France—this time with the blue, white, and red tricolor—in 1800. Then, on April 30, 1803, the United States purchased the sprawling Louisiana Territory from France's Napoléon Bonaparte. The new American flag then flew over a United States that was suddenly twice its previous size.

In 1810, colonists took control of land east of the Mississippi River that was part of Spain's West Florida Territory. Their flag was known as the Bonnie Blue. When Louisiana offically became a state in 1812, it was the eighteenth state to

join the Union. Its flag consisted of a star in a red square in the upper-left corner and thirteen alternating red, white, and blue horizontal stripes. During the Civil War, Louisiana changed its flag several times in 1861 and again in 1863. In 1912, the Louisiana State Legislature adopted the present flag. It is a blue banner, depicting a mother pelican in a nest with three young pelicans and the state motto, "Union, Justice, and Confidence." ■

Louisiana's State Seal

Louisiana's first territorial governor, William C. C. Claiborne, admired the eastern brown pelican, a large waterbird that lived along the Gulf Coast. He was impressed with the fact that the bird fed its young with pieces of its own flesh when food was scarce.

The governor depicted the pelican on all of his official correspondence. Many different versions of the bird were used—sometimes showing it sitting on a nest with as many as twelve chicks. In reality, the bird usually has three chicks at a time. So this version was adopted on April 30, 1902, in the official state seal. ■

Louisiana's State Songs

"You Are My Sunshine"

Words and Music by
Jimmy Davis and Charles Mitchell

The other night, dear
As I lay sleeping
I dreamed I held you in my arms
When I awoke, dear
I was mistaken
And I hung my head and cried;

You are my sunshine
My only sunshine
You make me happy
When skies are grey
You'll never know, dear
How much I love you
Please don't take my sunshine
*   away.* ■

"Give Me Louisiana"

Words by Doralice Fontane
Music by Dr. John Croom

Give me Louisiana,
The State where I was born
The State of snowy cotton,
The best I've ever known;
A State of sweet magnolias,
And Creole melodies.

Oh, give me Louisiana,
The State where I was born
Oh, what sweet old mem'ries
The mossy old oaks bring.
It brings us the story
of our Evangeline.

A State of old tradition,
of old plantation days
Makes good ole Louisiana
The sweetest of all States. ■

Louisiana's State Symbols

State amphibian: Green tree frog Also known as the fried bacon frog, the cowbell frog, and the bell frog, the green tree frog lives in swamps, bayous, and other damp areas.

State bird: Eastern brown pelican The pelican (top left) scoops up fish in its large bill and its pouch. A month-old pelican eats 5 pounds (2 kg) of fish a day! One of Louisiana's nicknames is the Pelican State.

State colors: Gold, white, and blue

State crustacean: Crawfish Although it resembles a small lobster, the crawfish varies in color. Louisiana is the crawfish capital of the world.

State dog: Catahoula leopard dog Louisiana's native breed is a cross between hunting dogs called catahoul (dogs of the clear water) by Native Americans and sixteenth-century Spanish war dogs. The dogs have webbed toes, making it easier for them to track game through swamps. They have a rough, spotted coat and milky-white, amber, or green eyes.

State flower: Magnolia The magnolia (bottom left) has large, creamy-white blossoms and a fragrant scent. The magnolia is an evergreen.

State fossil: Petrified palm-wood

State freshwater fish: White perch The white perch is also known as the sac-au-lait and white crappie.

State gemstone: Agate Agate is found in Louisiana gravel.

State insect: Honeybee (below) Honey has been collected in Louisiana since the early nineteenth century and is now among the state's major agricultural products.

State mammal: Black bear Intelligent, shy, and secretive, black bears try to avoid contact with humans. They range over large areas in search of food, such as berries, acorns, and honey.

State musical instrument: Diatonic accordion Commonly known as the Cajun accordion, this instrument was first introduced to Louisiana by German immigrants during the mid-1870s.

State reptile: Alligator Full-grown alligators resemble giant lizards and are dull gray and dark olive in color. They live in the waters and lowlands of Louisiana.

State tree: Bald cypress The bald cypress (right) grows well in swampy areas. Its durable wood is used for building houses and boats.

State wildflower: Louisiana iris The state wildflower, which ranges in color from pale blue to deep indigo, grows in Louisiana's damp, marshy regions.

The Parishes

The term *parish,* used instead of county in Louisiana, is a holdover from the state's days as a Spanish colony. *Parish* is actually a church term for administrative areas of the Roman Catholic Church. The constitution of 1845 instituted the parish system. There are sixty-four parishes in Louisiana, providing local services such as road repair and police protection. Most parishes have a "police jury," which acts like a county board of commissioners in other states and elects its own chairman or president. Parish officials are generally elected for a four-year term. Several parishes have a mayor and city-parish council local government.

Within the parishes are about three hundred cities, towns, and villages. A mayor, aided by a city council, handles the running of the community.

A lock on Bayou Plaquemine in Plaquemine Parish

Louisiana's parishes

The Democratic Party controlled Louisiana after Reconstruction—the rebuilding era of the Southern states that followed the Civil War—but the Republican Party grew much stronger in the 1970s. David C. Treen, elected in 1979, was the first Republican governor since 1877.

Local Leaders

Because of their wealth and connections, local leaders are often the powers behind the scenes in Louisiana. They may or may not hold office, but they control other office-holders. Leander Perez, nicknamed The Judge, was boss of Plaquemine Parish for decades. Although he was not elected to any office, he was a power in local politics from the 1930s to the 1960s. He advocated strict segregation, and it took the legal muscle of the federal government to break Perez's hold on his community. Perez was also excommunicated from the church by the Louisiana archbishop—a punishment that probably had more punch than the long arm of the federal law.

The Budget

Taxes pay for 40 percent of Louisiana's services for its citizens. Much of the rest of the state's operating budget comes from the U.S. government and from royalties (payments) for the use of mineral rights. In addition to an income tax, Louisianians pay a sales tax on purchases. Corporations also pay taxes.

The Right to Vote

Racist attitudes in Louisiana after Reconstruction prevented most blacks from exercising their rights as citizens. As a result of the high turnout of African-American voters in the 1896 elections, a convention was called in 1898 to disenfranchise, or take away the vote from, as many blacks as possible without violating the Fifteenth Amendment to the U.S. Constitution. The Fifteenth Amendment says that the rights of citizens to vote should not be denied because of race, color, or "previous condition of servitude." When Louisiana's racist policies took effect, however, only people who were able to read and write, who owned property valued at more than $300, and who could answer questions about certain historical events were eligible to vote.

To protect poor or illiterate whites, a "grandfather" clause was approved. It said that anyone who had voted on or before January 1, 1867, as well as his son and grandson, could vote. Even white foreigners who lived in the state for five years and were made citizens before 1898 were included. The restrictions were not lifted until the civil rights movement of the 1960s. ■

CHAPTER EIGHT

Business
Is Business

Louisiana's location in the South and its outlets to the Gulf of Mexico have made the state an economic powerhouse. The ranchlands of Texas lie to the west, the rich soil of Mississippi to the east, and the farmlands of Arkansas to the north. The Mississippi River system ties it all together.

The Mississippi River, with tributaries such as the Red River, shaped Louisiana both geographically and economically. Its waters deposited silt on the delta, creating rich wetlands, and its waterways make up a natural transportation system. The Native Americans were the first to use the rivers as trade routes, carrying goods upstream, downstream, and throughout the South. From the beginning of European settlement, commercial traffic kept the waterways bustling.

Port of New Orleans

Villages Grow to Cities

Villages along the waterways grew into towns and then into cities. Tens of thousands of jobs are tied to the river, from deckhands to grocery-store clerks, from mechanics to marketing directors. Port-related businesses spend an estimated $11.4 billion in Louisiana.

Opposite: Dock-workers at Baily's Seafood in Cameron wait for the next shrimp boat to arrive.

Boats and Barges

A single river barge can carry 1,500 tons of cargo, about the same load that 15 railcars or 60 semitrailer trucks can handle. Tugs and towboats can push or pull from one to fifty of these heavy barges at a time. The towboat and its barges are called a tow. ▪

By the late 1990s, Louisiana ranked first in the United States for waterborne tonnage.

A Major Port

The Port of New Orleans has 22 miles (35 km) of loading and unloading facilities, the world's longest continuous cargo complex. The port regulates 88 miles (141 km) of private and public waterfront property, with fifty major docking spots. Every year, more than 2,500 vessels dock at New Orleans, and more than 100,000 barges move through the city each year.

Port of New Orleans

New Orleans gets cargo from around the world, mainly in strong metal containers that are easily loaded on truck beds or railcars. On some docks, trains can pull up right next to the ships. Steel, heavy machinery, vehicles, rubber, and many other goods are handled this way.

Fuel oil, gas, and other liquid cargo flow from ship to shore, or vice versa, through giant hoses. Grain from the northern states arrives on barges for storage in tall buildings called grain elevators prior to being shipped overseas. Fast-moving conveyor belts load corn, wheat, oats, and barley into the freighters registered in a variety of countries.

Shipbuilders

Avondale Shipyards builds minesweepers, transports, and tankers. It ranked as the largest private employer in Louisiana during the 1990s, with 5,200 skilled workers. Located 5 miles (8 km) from the city of New Orleans business district, Avondale is one of the largest U.S. shipbuilders. Some of the vessels constructed for the U.S. Navy cost $100 million each.

River Pilots

The Coast Guard licenses the pilots who guide towboats and other vessels along the rivers. Some pilots are qualified for several stretches of a tricky waterway while others concentrate on a single area. For example, one pilot may take a freighter from the Gulf of Mexico to Pilottown, Louisiana, inside the mouth of the Mississippi River. Another pilot takes the ship from Pilottown to New Orleans, and a third pilot then guides the ship from New Orleans to Baton Rouge. ■

What Louisiana Grows, Manufactures, and Mines

Agriculture	Manufacturing	Mining
Cotton	Chemicals	Natural gas
Beef cattle	Petroleum products	Petroleum
Sugarcane	Transportation equipment	
Soybeans	Paper products	
Milk		
Rice		

Bags of flour being loaded onto a ship docked at the Port of Lake Charles

Leading Ports

The Port of South Louisiana—midway between New Orleans and Baton Rouge—is the nation's leading port in tonnage, handling almost 185 million tons of cargo per year. The port's 205-acre (83-ha) Globalplex Intermodel Terminal handles everything from limestone to natural gas. It is an industrial complex, too, with fertilizer and chemical plants, sugar and oil refineries, and a steel-processing plant.

Baton Rouge, which ranks fourth in the United States in tonnage, moves more than 86 million tons of cargo per year. Louisiana's next major port, the Port of Lake Charles, ranks twelfth in the nation, handling 48 million tons of cargo per year. Some of the state's smaller ports serve specialized markets. For example, the Port of St. Bernard, a few miles downstream from New Orleans, serves the textile industry.

Linked to the World

Louisiana has economic links around the globe. Its business executives deal with companies in Europe, Asia, Australia, and South America. The state encourages foreign trade by organizing trade missions to Brazil, Germany, Canada, and other countries.

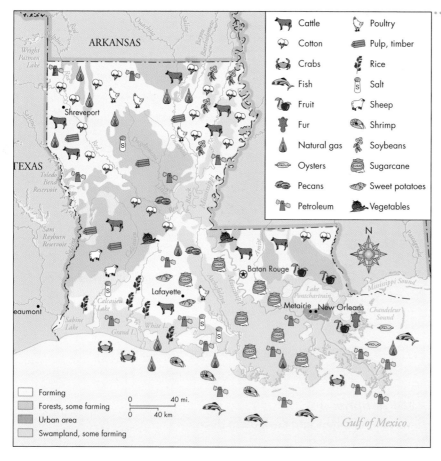

Map legend:
- Cattle
- Cotton
- Crabs
- Fish
- Fruit
- Fur
- Natural gas
- Oysters
- Pecans
- Petroleum
- Poultry
- Pulp, timber
- Rice
- Salt
- Sheep
- Shrimp
- Soybeans
- Sugarcane
- Sweet potatoes
- Vegetables

- Farming
- Forests, some farming
- Urban area
- Swampland, some farming

0   40 mi.
0   40 km

On the Farms

Louisiana produces a wide variety of crops, from cotton to sweet potatoes. The northern part of the state grows oats, alfalfa, potatoes, strawberries, and peaches, and many small farms produce cabbages, eggplants, tomatoes, spinach, and other vegetables. In the southern half of the state, rice and cotton are big crops along the Mississippi River. Rice is also grown along the southwest Gulf Coast. Rice was first grown in Louisiana in the early eighteenth century and exported to Europe by 1750. Irrigation projects helped open up new paddies (rice fields) in the prairie regions of the state. In 1996, sod farms cultivated 2,923 acres (1,183 ha) of turf

Hot Stuff

Crystal Hot Sauce, made in New Orleans since 1923, is carried by freighter to seventy-five countries. One of its customers is Saudi Arabia, a desert country whose citizens love the fiery food flavoring as much as Louisianians do. ■

Red Beans and Rice

Here's a simple recipe for one of the many spicy Cajun dishes popular in Louisiana.

Ingredients:

    1 lb. dried red kidney beans

            oil

        1 large onion, chopped

        1 green pepper, chopped

        4 celery stalks, chopped

        4 cloves of garlic, minced

        1 smoked ham hock

1/2–1 lb. sliced andouille sausage (or a
            similar smoked sausage)

        1 bay leaf

            salt, cayenne, and black pepper to taste

            Tabasco or other hot sauce to taste

Directions:

Wash the beans and soak them overnight.

Drain the beans and put enough fresh water in the pot to completely cover them. Boil, making sure the beans are always covered with water, for 45–60 minutes or until the beans are tender.

Meanwhile, sauté the onion, green pepper, and celery in the oil until the onions are clear. Add the garlic and sauté for 1 minute.

Drain and return the beans to the pot. Add the vegetable mixture and the ham hock, sausage, bay leaf, cayenne, black pepper, salt, hot sauce, and enough water to cover the mixture.

Boil, then reduce temperature and simmer, stirring occasionally, for about 3 hours, until the mixture is thick. Mash the beans while they're cooking for added thickness.

Serve over hot white rice, with added hot sauce to taste.

grass to be used for landscaping. In the same year, more than eight hundred growers cultivated 377,192 acres (152,644 ha) of sugarcane, producing more than 10 million tons of cane.

Cotton was introduced to Louisiana in 1718 by Emanuel Prudhomme on his plantation just outside Natchitoches. It was not grown extensively until 1793, after the invention of the cotton gin, a machine that separated cotton from the seeds and hull. Today, about 890,000 acres (360,170 ha) of the state are used for cotton cultivation. The cotton fields are regularly rotated with corn to ensure that the soil remains fertile.

These handpicked strawberries will be used to make wine.

The Centennial Pecan

The first scientific cultivation of pecans was recorded in 1846 on Telesphore J. Roman's Oak Alley Plantation in St. James Parish. Antoine, one of the plantation's slave gardeners, developed a new strain of pecans called Centennial. ■

Farmers—Past and Future

Agriculture has long been a major part of life in Louisiana. Today, the Louisiana Farm Bureau's Young Farmers and Ranchers program helps growers keep up with the latest techniques in agriculture and product marketing. Four-H and the Future Farmers of America are also popular among young people in rural areas.

There was no such support in the early days. Before the Civil War, most of the state's agricultural products came from plantations. Every plantation had a main building where the owner and his family lived, as well as many outbuildings.

The typical plantation had 7 to 25 slaves. A few had 50 or more slaves, and Houmas House, with 1,000, was the largest plantation. Most slaves worked in the fields, a few were house servants, and others were skilled blacksmiths or carpenters. The proximity of these Louisiana plantations to New Orleans, the world's largest cotton market before the Civil War, was a definite advantage. Many growers became millionaires.

After the Civil War, former slaves often worked for large landowners who also owned the local stores and most forms of transportation. Even a farmer who owned his land was usually dependent on the "boss" to buy his products and ship his goods. Small farmers often had to share their produce with the landowner to pay the rent on both their homes and their land, as well as to buy necessities in the neighborhood store. This system, called "sharecropping," gave landowners control over small farmers. ■

Farm-raised alligators being released into the wetlands

Aquaculture Includes Alligators

The seafood industry is a big business in Louisiana. Aquaculture products range from crawfish to alligators. About 87 percent of the 50,000 tons of crawfish produced annually for sale in the United States comes from Louisiana. They come from both natural wetlands and from culture ponds. The largest foreign market for the United States is Sweden, which imports 2,500 tons of crawfish a year.

Fishing

Freshwater fisheries are also important to Louisiana's economy. To prevent overfishing, the state's Wildlife and Fisheries Department started a licensing system in 1995. In 1996, the crawfish catch was 19.5 million pounds (8.8 million kg) compared with 41.1 million pounds (18.6 million kg) the previous year.

Not Just a Pretty Face

A wild channel catfish can weigh up to 50 pounds (23 kg) and live up to fifteen years. A farmed channel catfish is harvested in eighteen months, when it weighs about 1.5 pounds (0.7 kg). There are four families and twenty-eight species of catfish in the United States, including the sweet-tasting channel cat, the most popular. ■

Oyster harvesters and crabbers have been hit hard by high fuel costs for their boats, and environmental concerns along the coasts have placed some areas offlimits. Also, pollution problems along some sections of the Gulf make the catch dangerous to eat.

Varied Industries

Louisiana is also an industrial powerhouse. As the third-largest refiner of petroleum products in the United States, the state produces 25 percent of all the country's petrochemicals. Plants around the state also produce paper and wood products, offshore drilling

Offshore oil platform in the Gulf of Mexico off the coast of Louisiana

Second Chances

Companies in Louisiana can take advantage of two free training programs for their workers. The QuickStart Training Program uses the state's fifty vocational-technical schools to provide job training tailored to meet the employer's requirements. The schools can also set up on-the-job training. The second program is part of the federally funded Job Training Partnership Act, which provides money to educate workers who have lost their jobs or want additional skills. Programs such as these will ensure that Louisiana's workforce of 1.9 million is ready for the future. With the support of the state's unions, which represent about 16 percent of the workforce, Louisiana's companies are geared for the turn of the century. ■

and aerospace equipment, as well as communications gear and amphibious vehicles. Louisiana is also America's largest manufacturer of gold rings and automobile headlights.

This broad mix of industries makes manufacturing the largest part of the state's $800-billion-a-year economy. By the end of the 1990s, the economic problems of the previous decade seemed like a bad dream. Investments were rising, with tax incentives to fuel the economy and strong environmental policies to protect the state's resources.

Several university-affiliated facilities keep Louisiana abreast of new technologies and methods in medicine, business, and environmental concerns. They include the Biomedical Research Institute of Northwest Louisiana, which focuses on heart disease, and the Louisiana Universities Marine Consortium, which studies wetlands and the Gulf Coast. This combination of resources, productivity, markets, transportation, incentives, and lifestyle ensures Louisiana's continued growth.

CHAPTER NINE

Louisiana: A People Place

Louisiana has one of the most diverse populations in the United States. Before we can understand today's Louisianians, however, we need to step back in history. It is important to know the difference between a Cajun and a Creole. These terms are often used to describe all of Louisiana's residents, but they properly refer to people from the southern part of the state.

Historically, Creoles were descendants of early Spanish or French settlers and African slaves. The word *Creole* comes from the Spanish word *criollo,* meaning "white child born in the colonies."

Some of Louisiana's Creoles are descendants of former African slaves.

Creole Traditions

Historically, the Creoles were the wealthy upper class in early Louisiana. They spoke French and educated their children in France. French opera, theater, cooking, and literature were considered the height of civilization. Today, Creole families enjoy *reveillon* on Christmas and New Year's Eve—a celebration that includes religious services followed by a midnight supper. Relatives and friends go from house to house to eat, sing, and dance. During the holiday season, visitors sample the Creole dishes served in elegant gourmet restaurants.

Opposite: Sailors on leave taking photographs by an outdoor mural in New Orleans

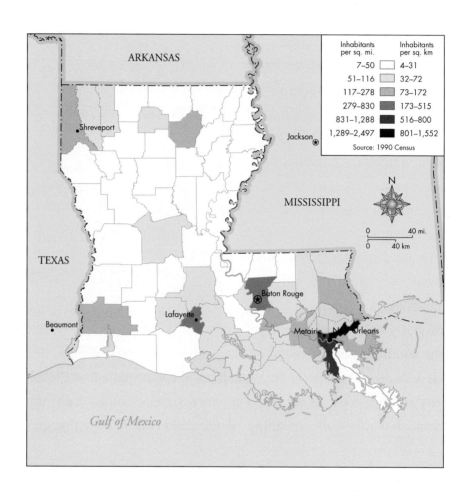

Louisiana's population density

Inhabitants per sq. mi. | Inhabitants per sq. km
7–50 | 4–31
51–116 | 32–72
117–278 | 73–172
279–830 | 173–515
831–1,288 | 516–800
1,289–2,497 | 801–1,552

Source: 1990 Census

ARKANSAS

Shreveport

Jackson

MISSISSIPPI

TEXAS

Baton Rouge

Lafayette

Beaumont

Metairie   New Orleans

Gulf of Mexico

Holiday Bonfires

According to tradition, Papa Noël, the Creole Santa Claus, finds his way to New Orleans by following the lights of bonfires along the Mississippi River. For weeks prior to the holidays, families who live along the river build large statues out of wood and kindling. On Christmas Eve, they set fire to the wood, creating a long line of blazing figures. Visitors from around the world travel by bus or steamboat tours to see the fiery display. The line of blazing fires can be seen for miles along the levees, creating a festive atmosphere. ■

The Acadians

Cajuns are descendants of the Acadians—the French Canadians who lived in Nova Scotia as early as 1604. Their land was so fertile that they called it *L'Acadie,* meaning "heaven on Earth." In 1713, after a war with France, Britain seized control of Canada. The Acadians refused to swear allegiance to the English king and in 1755 were evicted from their homes. In 1765, Acadian leader Joseph Brossard arrived in Louisiana with 200 of his family and friends. More than 10,000 other Acadians eventually followed. Through the years, the word *Acadian* evolved into *Cajun.* Many cultures have merged to make today's Cajun population, but about 1 million Louisianians trace their ancestry back to the original Acadians.

Cajuns in historic Acadian Village, Lafayette

The African-Americans

One of the major influences on Louisiana came from slaves brought from the West African coast. Many of these men and women were fishers, farmers, cooks, and cattlebreeders, and they brought their skills with them.

In 1806, legislation was passed to prevent free blacks from entering the Territory of Orleans from Santo Domingo (now the Dominican Republic and Haiti) and other Caribbean islands. In 1807, the entry of any free black into the colony was blocked. The importation of slaves had increased, however, and by 1809, 112,000 Africans were brought to Louisiana each year. Most were "sold upriver," meaning that they were sent to Southern plantations. (The phrase is still used today, meaning "betrayed.")

In addition to the African slaves, more than ten thousand other French-speaking blacks arrived between 1809 and 1810. They left the war-torn island of Santo Domingo during a slave revolt. This massive influx of black freedmen and slaves left a Caribbean imprint on southern Louisiana. Many of these people were educated teachers, writers, and entertainers, as well as craft workers.

Today's black residents of Louisiana have become renowned in many walks of life. New Orleans mayor Marc Morial, Air

The Amistad Research Center at Tulane University, New Orleans

Force general Bernard E. Randolph, and basketball star Nat "Sweetwater" Clifton of the Harlem Globetrotters are among them. The Amistad Research Center in Tulane University has thousands of documents that record the experience of black men and women in Louisiana from the eighteenth century to modern times.

The Germans and Swiss

Many of the Germans and Swiss who arrived in Louisiana around 1718 were lured to this rugged frontier by land developer John Law. Most of these settlers came from the picturesque Rhine River Valley, which had been devastated by the Thirty Years' War (1618–1648). Europe was slowly recovering from that conflict when Law's agents arrived with their German-language pamphlets trumpeting the riches of the New World. They convinced entire families to leave their homeland and sail across the ocean in search of a better life.

In 1721, a large group of German immigrants found themselves in the wilderness 25 miles (40 km) north of New Orleans. They began building houses and planting crops. More settlers followed. They were called the Redemptorists, because they were able to repay the debt incurred for their ocean voyage by working as blacksmiths, carpenters, and bricklayers.

Eventually, this area had so many German settlers that it became known as *La Côte des Allemands* (the German Coast). German names eventually became less common, however, because the priests who recorded baptisms, marriages, and deaths were

Longtime Mayor

Martin Behrman (at center) was the first German mayor of New Orleans. A hardworking vote-getter for the local Democratic party, Behrman rose through the ranks at City Hall and was elected mayor in 1904. He also headed the so-called Choctaw Club of Louisiana—a group of politicians who ran New Orleans from behind the scenes.

Despite demands for reform, Behrman was reelected in 1908 and held office for three more terms until finally losing an election in 1920. That loss was not enough to keep this hardy politician down. Behrman was reelected in 1925. He died the following year, having held the office of New Orleans mayor longer than anyone else ever had. ■

French. The German name *Weber* became *Webre* or *Fabre* and *Traeger* became *Tregre*. Between 1848 and 1900, the Germans were the largest group of foreign-language speakers in Louisiana.

The Italians

Italians have played important roles in Louisiana's history. In the late sixteenth century, an Italian soldier named Henri (Enrico) de Tonti was second in command to René-Robert Cavelier, Sieur de la Salle, when the French explorer came down the Mississippi River. Tonti was the major European contact with the Native Americans and laid the ground for settlement of the colony. In 1699, Tonti sailed around the Gulf of Mexico, mapping the entire area. He became governor of the French-controlled Mississippi River Delta region.

By the 1850s, Louisiana had the largest population of Italians in the United States. Immigrant Angelo Socola improved rice-growing techniques on his farm. He also built processing plants that launched one of the state's most important industries.

A street vendor selling garlic and melons in New Orleans

The Italians who came to Louisiana in the late nineteenth and early twentieth centuries settled in the French Quarter. Many were natives of Sicily, an island off the coast of the Italian peninsula. They were proud people whose benevolent associations provided them with free health care and other social services. Mother Cabrini, a Catholic nun born in Lombardy, built schools and day-care centers in New Orleans and spread her educational message around the United States. In 1946, she became the first U.S. citizen to be canonized as a saint in the Roman Catholic Church.

The Spanish and Hispanics

The French Quarter in New Orleans should have been called the Spanish Quarter. It was constructed by the Spanish settlers who were the first to colonize Louisiana. As a reminder of that heritage, street names in the Quarter are given both in French and Spanish. Today, the only Louisianians who can trace their heritage directly

Street sign on Calle San Felipe in the French Quarter

back to Spain are the descendants of a group of Spanish-speaking Canary Islanders who settled in St. Bernard Parish in 1778.

Thousands of Hispanics from throughout Central and South America and the Caribbean now call Louisiana their home. They are a multinational group, coming from Nicaragua, the Dominican Republic, Honduras, Cuba, and other countries. Many came to work in the banana business or to flee oppression. The Cervantes Foundation of Hispanic Art in New Orleans promotes their art, theater, and literature, and the Hispanic Cultural Coalition sponsors programs such as Fiesta Americana.

The Asians

Asians have lived in Louisiana since the eighteenth century. Spanish-speaking sailors from the Philippines jumped ship in Mexico and, after many harrowing adventures, reached southern Louisiana. In the nineteenth century, hundreds of Chinese came to the state as contract laborers. They worked in the rice fields and on the railroads to pay for their passage to America. Most remained in Louisiana and became successful business leaders.

Harry Lee, a prominent ChineseAmerican, was elected sheriff of Jefferson Parish in 1980 and served several terms. He was known as the Chinese Cowboy because he always wore a cowboy hat and boots.

Population of Louisiana's Major Cities (1990)

New Orleans	496,938
Baton Rouge	219,531
Shreveport	198,525
Metairie	149,248
Lafayette	80,352
Appleton	94,440

Tina Soon, a journalist born in Shanghai, is another well-known Louisianian. Her weekly column "On the Rim" appears in the *Times-Picayune,* New Orleans's major newspaper.

The Irish

The Irish have also left their mark on Louisiana. Irish soldiers of fortune served with Jean-Baptiste Le Moyne, Sieur de Bienville, when he explored the area. In 1781, another Louisiana Irishman, Oliver Pollock, donated his fortune to fund the Spanish army that defeated the English in the Battle of Pensacola.

Irish laborers built the 6-mile (10-km) New Basin Canal that links Lake Pontchartrain with the Mississippi River. They worked for 50 cents a day, plus room, board, and an extra $6.25 a month for

Sunset over Lake Pontchartrain

whiskey. It was a difficult, dangerous job, and at least 8,000 Irish workers died of illness and injury while constructing the canal.

The next wave of Irish immigrants settled in the Irish Channel, now a trendy neighborhood along the river, complete with galleries, boutiques, and coffeehouses. The New Orleans Irish celebrate St. Patrick's Day in parades through the French Quarter.

School Days

This great ethnic mix comes together in Louisiana's schools, enabling students to learn about and understand many other cultures. Ursuline nuns fostered the education of Louisiana's children in the eighteenth and nineteenth centuries. The state's first school, founded by Capuchin friars in 1725, had seven pupils. The first public school opened in 1772. Today, 2,300 private schools and 66 public-school districts throughout the state accommodate about

Loyola University in New Orleans

793,000 pupils. Of that number, 366,000 children are black, 10,000 are Asian, 9,000 are Hispanic, 5,000 are Native American, and the remainder are white.

Several schools help children with special needs, including the Louisiana School for the Deaf in Baton Rouge. At the Louisiana School for Math, Science and the Arts in Natchitoches, high-school students live on a campus, as college students do. Pupils can select courses in eight languages, calculus, literary analysis, and film animation, in addition to history, sociology, English, and other traditional courses.

College Bound

After high school, students can attend one of the state's forty-four technical schools to study agricultural techniques, banking, forest technology, health care, and a wide range of other specialized subjects. For more specific studies, 154 private schools teach such subjects as floral design, electronics, and diamond cutting. A student can even learn to be a gourmet chef or an able-bodied sailor. At Louisiana Tech University in Ruston, students concentrate on math, engineering, and computer skills.

As part of its higher-education system, Louisiana has twenty four-year public, fifteen four-year private, and six two-year colleges and universities. There are thirteen prominent schools in the Louisiana Association of Independent Colleges and Universities, including the nationally known Tulane University. Louisiana also has several well-known schools for blacks, such as Dillard University, founded in 1869. Xavier University is the only black college among America's 235 Catholic colleges.

Chancellor Dolores Spike

Dolores Spike, chancellor of Southern University in Baton Rouge from 1988 to 1991, was the first black woman in the United States to head a major liberal-arts college. The school is the state's largest black university. ▇

CHAPTER TEN

Culture
Everywhere

Louisianians live by the philosophy of *joie de vivre,* meaning the "joy of living." The cities are full of cultural events and entertainment. Music—ranging from jazz, rock, and Cajun to rap, salsa, and classical—is at the heart of it all.

In the early eighteenth century, New Orleans already had its own opera company, the first in North America. Today, music lovers rush to buy the latest Blood and Grits "swamp jazz" CD on the Bymymamas label, one of Louisiana's record companies.

A musician playing a Dobro, a type of acoustic guitar with a metal resonator

Jazz and Blues

Jazz is among the best known of Louisiana's many musical styles. Its origins are in Italian brass-band percussion and African rhythms. Stars such as Louis "Satchmo" Armstrong, Jelly Roll Morton, Louis Prima, and the Marsalis family added their own special touches to the form. Thousands of international visitors attend the New Orleans Jazz & Heritage Festival and similar events in Louisiana each year.

A wonderful jazz tradition is still honored at funerals in New Orleans. After the slow, sad "first line" leaves the cemetery, the mourners parade home in a joyous "second line," led by a band. Onlookers join the clapping, singing, and parasol-twirling crowd in celebration of the life of the deceased person.

The blues were born in Louisiana with the soulful sound of Delta farmworkers and then spread throughout America. Father of

Piano Prodigy

Shreveport's Van Cliburn was the first American to win the prestigious international Tchaikovsky piano competition in the former Soviet Union. He won the title in 1958 when he was only twenty-four years old. ■

Opposite: A trombone player in Jackson Square, New Orleans

the blues Huddie "Leadbelly" Ledbetter is buried near his hometown of Mooringsport. Rock-and-roll stars Fats Domino and Huey "Piano" Smith were also born in Louisiana.

From Gospel to Dixie

At any church in Louisiana you can hear the best in gospel song, accompanied by drums, tambourines, piano, and organ. Classical music lovers can attend a performance of the Sinfonietta of Baton Rouge or the Shreveport Symphony.

The *Lousiana Hayride* was one of America's most popular radio shows a generation ago, leading the way in country-western programming. Today, the *Dixie Jamboree,* aired from Ruston, presents the music of popular country stars.

Parties and Parades

New Orleans loves festivals. It seems like there is a street party on every corner at all hours of the night and day. But Mardi Gras remains the most exciting event of the year. Parades and fancy-dress balls begin two weeks before Fat Tuesday (the English translation of *Mardi Gras*). Long ago, in Europe's Catholic countries, a fatted calf was paraded through the streets on the Tuesday before Ash Wednesday, the day on which the religious season of Lent begins.

During Mardi Gras processions, costumed paraders toss plastic beads and other trinkets to the watching crowds. *Krewes,* or clubs, sponsor the parades and build the marvelous floats. Each krewe works for an entire year to prepare for the event.

A float in the Mardi Gras parade along St. Charles Street in New Orleans

A man stirs a giant pot of gumbo at the Bridge City Gumbo Festival

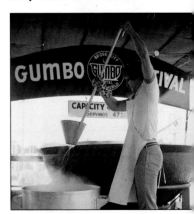

Mardi Gras Gallop

The Courir du Mardi Gras is a country-style Mardi Gras in which costumed riders gallop from farm to farm collecting ingredients for a giant gumbo—a Creole stew. The riders are accompanied by Cajun bands traveling on flatbed trucks. The inhabitants of each farmhouse along the way contribute a few chickens or vegetables for the community feast.

The first movie filmed in Louisiana was *Faust* (1908). The first of the Tarzan movies was filmed in Morgan City in 1917. ∎

In the Movies

Dozens of movies have been filmed in Louisiana. With its plantations, riverboats, and lively cities, it is a set designer's dream.

Historic Nachitoches provided backdrops for the Civil War epic *Horse Soldiers* (1959) and *Steel Magnolias* (1988). *The Big Easy* (1985) and *Interview with a Vampire* (1993) were also filmed in New Orleans.

Art and Artists

John James Audubon, author of *Birds of America*

The first artist to show his work in Louisiana was A. de Batz in 1732. The subjects of his paintings were the region's Native Americans. Today's art scene includes the famous *Blue Dog* series by Cajun artist George Rodrigue, as well as the work of hundreds of other contemporary artists.

Louisiana's notable artist Clementine Hunter died in 1987 at age 102. Once a plantation field hand and cook, she took up painting in her forties and became known for her vibrant colors and expressive portraits.

The painter John James Audubon worked for years in Louisiana during the nineteenth century. His work, published in many books, including *Birds of America* (1838), captured the likenesses of the state's feathered species. Audubon State Park and Commemorative Area in the St. Francisville area and Audubon

Park and Zoological Gardens in New Orleans are named after this important wildlife artist.

Some of Louisiana's artists have used unusual materials. New Orleans sculptor Lucien Marcon made figures out of wax in the 1850s, and several stonecutters carved a statue out of a 10-foot (3-m)-high pillar of salt for the Cotton Exposition in 1884.

Books and Authors

Colonists published works about Louisiana as early as the sixteenth century, although the books were printed in Europe. The colony set up its first printing press in 1764. As late as the 1850s, most books printed in Louisiana were in French. *Les Cenelles* (1845), a collection of love songs by African-Americans, was the first such anthology in the United States.

Playwright Lillian Hellman, who was born in New Orleans, won international acclaim for her dramatic plays, including *The Children's Hour* (1934) and *The Little Foxes* (1939).

Many famous writers who visited Louisiana have been inspired by its dark bayous, its charming towns, and its rainbow of people. *Life on the Mississippi* by Mark Twain (Samuel Clemens) includes accounts of his trips to New Orleans, and Winston

Playwright Lillian Hellman

Scene from Tennessee Williams's *A Streetcar Named Desire* starring Marlon Brando and Vivien Leigh

Churchill, prime minister of Britain, wrote about Louisiana after his visits to the state.

A Prizewinning Classic

A Streetcar Named Desire (1947) by Mississippi-born Tennessee Williams is one of the most famous plays about life in the South. The Pulitzer Prize winner is set in the steamy French Quarter of New Orleans. In 1951, it was made into a classic movie starring Marlon Brando, Vivien Leigh, Kim Hunter, and Karl Malden.

Sports Center

During the late nineteenth century, New Orleans was the boxing capital of the United States. The longest match in America was a 110-rounder that lasted 7 hours and 19 minutes, ending in a draw. It was fought between Andy Brown and Jack Burke on April 6, 1893.

The state's many other firsts include a world's auto record established by Ralph DePalma in 1909 when he drove 50 miles (80 km) around a dirt track in New Orleans—at a speed of 60 miles (96 km) per hour.

Louisiana's sports heroes range from motorcycle racer Freddie Spencer to tennis star Kay McDaniel. In 1988, weight lifter Leigh Ann Lloyd Legg set an American record by lifting a combined total

The Superdome

The Louisiana Superdome looms above from the New Orleans skyline. The twenty-seven-story structure seats more than 95,000 patrons under a dome that covers almost 10 acres (4 ha), making it the largest enclosed stadium in the world. The top of the building is 273 feet (83 m) above the football field. Even the cost of the Superdome was super—$163 million by the time it was completed in 1975. ■

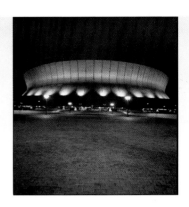

of 2,807 pounds (1,273 kilograms) in the squat, bench press, and dead lift divisions. Legg weighed only 121 pounds (55 kilograms) at the time!

Louisianians know how to enjoy themselves. "Let the good times roll" is the Louisiana way of life.

Jazz musicians in the French Quarter

Timeline

United States History

The first permanent British settlement is established in North America at Jamestown. **1607**

Pilgrims found Plymouth Colony, the second permanent British settlement. **1620**

America declares its independence from England. **1776**

The Treaty of Paris officially ends the Revolutionary War in America. **1783**

The U.S. Constitution is written. **1787**

The Louisiana Purchase almost doubles the size of the United States. **1803**

U.S and Britain **1812–15** fight the War of 1812.

Louisiana State History

1541 Hernando de Soto becomes the first European to see the Mississippi.

1682 René-Robert Cavelier, Sieur de La Salle, claims the Louisiana Territory for France.

1718 New Orleans is founded and named for Philippe II, Duc d'Orléans.

1722 New Orleans becomes the capital of Louisiana.

1724 The Black Code, which restricts movements of blacks around the colony, becomes law.

1764 Acadian immigrants arrive from Canada.

1800 Spain gives Louisiana back to France in the Treaty of San Ildefonso.

1803 The United States purchases Louisiana from Napoleon.

1812 Louisiana is admitted to the Union as the 18th state.

1815 Battle of New Orleans is won by General Andrew Jackson, defeating the British.

1835 Shreveport is founded.

1849 Baton Rouge becomes the capital of Louisiana.

United States History

The North and South fight each **1861–65** other in the American Civil War.

The United States is **1917–18** involved in World War I.

The stock market crashes, **1929** plunging the United States into the Great Depression.

The United States fights in **1941–45** World War II.

The United States becomes a **1945** charter member of the United Nations.

The United States fights **1951–53** in the Korean War.

The U.S. Congress enacts a series of **1964** groundbreaking civil rights laws.

The United States **1964–73** engages in the Vietnam War.

The United States and other **1991** nations fight the brief Persian Gulf War against Iraq.

Louisiana State History

1861 Louisiana secedes from the Union.

1868 Louisiana is accepted back into the Union.

1901 The first oil in Louisiana is discovered.

1909 Commercial mining of sulfur begins near Sulphur.

1927 The worst flood in U.S. history leaves 300,000 people homeless.

1935 Governor Huey Long assassinated in Baton Rouge at the state capitol.

1960 Two public schools in Orleans Parish are desegregated.

1975 The Louisiana Superdome is completed in New Orleans.

1978 Ernest N. "Dutch" Morial becomes New Orleans's first black mayor.

1984 Louisiana World's Fair is held in New Orleans.

Fast Facts

The capitol

Statehood date	April 30, 1812, the 18th state
Origin of state name	Named by Sieur de La Salle for King Louis XIV of France
State capital	Baton Rouge
State nickname	Pelican State
State motto	Union, Justice, and Confidence
State amphibian	Green tree frog
State bird	Eastern brown pelican
State colors	Gold, white, and blue
State crustacean	Crawfish
State dog	Catahoula leopard dog
State flower	Magnolia
State fossil	Petrified palmwood
State freshwater fish	White perch
State gemstone	Agate
State insect	Honeybee
State mammal	Black bear

Magnolia

Alligator

Kisatchie Bayou

Bayou Cocodrie
swamp

State musical instrument	Diatonic accordion
State reptile	Alligator
State songs	"Give Me Louisiana," words by Doralice Fontane and music by Dr. John Croom; "You Are My Sunshine," words and music by Jimmy H. Davis and Charles Mitchell
State tree	Bald cypress
State wildflower	Louisiana iris
State fair	Shreveport (October)
Total area; rank	49,650 sq. mi. (128,593 sq km); 31st
Land; rank	43,566 sq. mi. (112,835 sq km); 33rd
Water; rank	6,084 sq. mi. (15,757 sq km); 6th
Inland water; rank	4,153 sq. mi. (10,756 sq km); 5th
Coastal water; rank	1,931 sq. mi. (5,001 sq km); 3rd
Geographic center	Avoyelles, 3 miles (5 km) southeast of Marksville
Latitude and longitude	Louisiana is located approximately between 28° 00' and 33° 00' N and 89° 00' and 94° 00' W.
Highest point	Driskill Mountain, 535 feet (163 m)
Lowest point	–5 feet (–1.5 m) at New Orleans
Largest city	New Orleans
Number of parishes (counties)	64

Salt domes

Longest river	Mississippi River, 305 miles (491 km) in Louisiana out of a total length of 2,340 miles (3,766 km)
Population; rank	4,238,216 (1990 census); 21st
Density	89 persons per sq. mi. (34 per sq km)
Population distribution	68% urban, 32% rural
Ethnic distribution (does not equal 100%)	White 67.28% African-American 30.79% Hispanic 2.2% Asian and Pacific Islanders 0.97% Other 0.52% Native American 0.44%
Record high temperature	114°F (46°C) at Plain Dealing on August 10, 1936
Record low temperature	–16°F (–27°C) at Minden on February 13, 1899
Average July temperature	82°F (28°C)
Average January temperature	50°F (10°C)
Average yearly precipitation	57 inches (145 cm)

Poverty Point

A small lake near Kisatchie National Forest

Louisiana's Natural Areas

National Monument

Poverty Point National Monument commemorates a culture that thrived during the first and second millennia B.C.

National Military Park

Vicksburg National Military Park commemorates the site of the forty-seven-day siege that ended with the surrender of New Orleans to Union troops during the American Civil War.

National Historic Park

Jean Lafitte National Historical Park and Preserve was established to preserve the rich cultural heritage of Louisiana's delta region.

Cane River Creole National Historical Park contains significant sites, structures, and landscapes associated with the Creole culture.

New Orleans Jazz National Historical Park preserves the city's rich musical heritage.

National Forest

Kisatchie National Forest covers about 601,000 (243,216 ha) in north-central Louisiana.

State Forest

Alexander State Forest, the only state forest, is in central Louisiana.

State Parks

Louisiana's state park system consists of nearly 30 state parks, preservation areas, and commemorative areas.

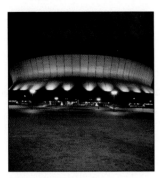
The Superdome

Sports Teams

NCAA Teams (Division 1)
Centenary College Gentlemen
Grambling State University Tigers
Louisiana State University Fighting Tigers
Louisiana Tech University Bulldogs
McNeese State University Cowboys
Nicholls State University Colonels
Northeast Louisiana University Indians
Southeastern Louisiana University Lions
Southern University–Baton Rouge Jaguars
Tulane University Green Wave
University of New Orleans Privateers
University of Southwestern Louisiana Ragin' Cajuns

National Football League
New Orleans Saints

Cultural Institutions

Libraries
The Louisiana State Library (Baton Rouge) provides information and books to the entire state.

Museums
Louisiana State Museum (New Orleans), Louisiana Historical Association (New Orleans) and Louisiana State Exhibit Museum (Shreveport) all house fine collections on the state and regional history.

The law school of
Louisiana State
University

Strawberries

Performing Arts

Louisiana has one major opera company and two major
symphony orchestras.

Universities and Colleges

In the mid-1990s, Louisiana had twenty public and thirteen
private institutions of higher learning.

Annual Events

January–March

Sugar Bowl Football Game in New Orleans (January)

Mardi Gras in New Orleans and many other cities
     (Shrove Tuesday)

Louisiana Black Heritage Festival in New Orleans (March)

Taste of the Bayou Food Festival in Houma (March)

Audubon Pilgrimage in St. Francisville (March)

April–June

Ponchatoula Strawberry Festival (April)

Holiday in Dixie in Shreveport (April)

Festival International de Louisiane in Lafayette (April)

Jazz and Heritage Festival in New Orleans (April–May)

Contraband Days in Lake Charles (May)

Tomato Festival in Chalmette (May)

Louisiana Peach Festival in Ruston (June)

Bayou Lacombe Crab Festival (June)

World Champion Pirogue Races in Lafitte (June)

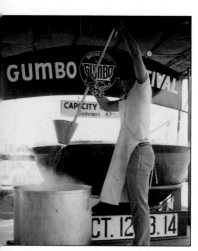

Bridge City Gumbo Festival

July–September

Tarpon Rodeo in Grand Isle (July)

Bayou Lafourche Antiques Show and Sale in Thibodaux (September)

Louisiana Shrimp and Petroleum Festival in Morgan City (September)

Festivals Acadiens in Lafayette (September)

Frog Festival in Rayne (September)

October–December

French Food Festival in Larose (October)

International Rice Festival in Crowley (October)

Louisiana State Fair in Shreveport (October)

Hodges Garden Fall Festival in Many (October)

Bridge City Gumbo Festival (October)

Gueydon Duck Festival (November)

Natchitoches Christmas Festival of Lights (December)

Bonfires on the Mississippi River Levee (December)

Famous People

Lillian Hellman

Louis Armstrong (1900–1971)	Musician
John James Audubon (1785–1851)	Ornithologist and artist
Pierre Gustav Toutant Beauregard (1818–1893)	Soldier
Arna Wendell Bontemps (1902–1973)	Author and poet
Truman Capote (1924–1984)	Author
Van Cliburn (1934–)	Classical musician
Fats Domino (1928–)	Musician
Lillian Hellman (1905–1984)	Playwright

Huey P. Long

Mahalia Jackson (1911–1972)	Gospel singer
Huddie "Leadbelly" Ledbetter (1888?–1949)	Folk singer and composer
Huey Pierce Long (1893–1935)	Politician
Wynton Marsalis (1961–)	Musician
Aaron Neville (1941–)	Musician
Paul Prudhomme (1940–)	Chef, author, and restaurateur
Edward Douglass White (1845–1921)	U.S. Supreme Court justice

To Find Out More

History

- Fraden, Dennis. *Louisiana.* Chicago: Childrens Press, 1995.

- Frois, Jeanne, and Larry Pardue (Illustrator). *Flags of Louisiana.* New Orleans: Pelican Publishing, 1995.

- Hintz, Martin. *Destination New Orleans.* Minneapolis: Lerner Publishing, 1997.

Biographies

- Frois, Jeanne, and Nathan B. Carley (Illustrator). *Louisianians All.* New Orleans: Pelican Publishing, 1992.

- De Varona, Frank, and Tom Redman (Illustrator). *Bernardo de Galvez.* Austin, Tex.: Raintree/Steck-Vaughn, 1989.

Websites

- **Louisiana State Home Page**
  http://www.state.la.us
  Information on all three branches of state and local government and links to information for students

- **Louisiana State Legislature**
  http://www.legis.state.la.us
  Information about laws, pending legislation, and governing bodies

- **What's Happen' Mardi! Louisiana's Family Attractions Newsletter**
  http://www.mardi.com
  Information about state parks, family attractions, plantations, special people, and links to other great Louisiana websites

Addresses

- **Louisiana Department of Natural Resources**
  Box 94396
  Baton Rouge, LA 70804-9396
  (504) 342-4500

- **Louisiana State Library**
  Box 131
  Baton Rouge, LA 70821-0131
  (504) 342-4913

- **Louisiana State Parks**
  Box 44426
  Baton Rouge, LA 70804-9291
  (888) 677-1400

- **State Museum of Louisiana**
  Box 2448
  New Orleans, LA 70176-2448
  (504) 568-6968

Index

Page numbers in *italics* indicate illustrations.

Meet the Author

Author Martin Hintz has written three books about New Orleans. He has often visited the state to research magazine articles.

Hintz's family often accompanied him on these trips. As little kids, Dan, Steve, and Kate Hintz were first entranced by the state when reading stories about the adventures of Gaston, a friendly alligator. Gaston lived in Louisiana's bayou country and had many adventures, such as attending Mardi Gras and riding on a float.

On their excursions, the Hintz family devoured mounds of steaming crawfish, visited the site of Evangeline's Oak, enjoyed outdoor jazz concerts, toured the state capital, and journeyed deep into bayou country on bird- and alligator-watching adventures.

Hintz, a nationally known travel writer, lives in Milwaukee, Wisconsin. He has written numerous titles in both the first and second Children's Press Enchantment of the World and America the

Beautiful series. He is a member of the Society of American Travel Writers. In 1998, Hintz headed a meeting in Lafayette, Louisiana's Cajun capital. Many of the state's conservation leaders, environmental activists, and government officials spoke at the meeting.

In addition to visiting Louisiana, Hintz used library resources, surfed the Internet, and talked with state officials on the telephone to gather information for this book.

Photo Credits